# Who Owns the Agent?

*Enterprise AI Accountability on the Microsoft Stack*

Sougata Roy

sougataroy.com

Who Owns the Agent? Enterprise AI Accountability on the Microsoft Stack



First edition, 2026. This edition reflects the Microsoft platform as verified against Microsoft documentation through August 2026. A second edition is planned for 2028.

Portions of this book adapt and extend the author's previously published work: the white paper Who Owns the Agent? (sougataroy.com, May 2026, DOI 10.5281/zenodo.20481551, CC BY 4.0) and The Authorization Layer framework library (Zenodo, July 2026, DOI 10.5281/zenodo.21245690, CC BY 4.0).

The arguments and frameworks in this book are the author's own, developed over several months in The Governance Gap newsletter and two prior publications. Shared industry vocabulary is identified as such. The author wrote the manuscript. Large language model tools were used for research assistance, for drafting assistance on some passages, and to revise and polish drafts. Factual claims were verified against named primary sources, editorial decisions were recorded in a production log kept throughout drafting, and the author reviewed and approved the final text.

Unless named and sourced, the organizations, scenes, and timelines in this book are illustrative constructions describing no particular employer, client, agency, or individual, and questions attributed to an examiner are the author's analytical framework, not any regulator's procedure. They are constructed from publicly available guidance, orders, decisions, and industry observations, and the incidents recounted are drawn from published primary sources named in the Sources section. Nothing in these pages draws on confidential or nonpublic information from the author's prior roles.

named vendor documentation on the dates shown and change on the vendor's schedule, not the author's.

ISBN: 979-8-9971983-0-5

For the person whose name goes on the signature line.

# Contents

# A Note on Capability Decay

This book describes a platform that changes faster than a book can. Feature boundaries move, license tiers get renamed, admin center screens are redrawn, and preview labels appear and clear on a cadence no print schedule survives. A book that staked its argument on those details would be wrong within a quarter, and several of the vendors covered here would not even be the ones to notice first.

The book handles this with a division of labor. Print carries what does not decay: the decisions organizations have to make, the records those decisions require, and the questions an examiner will ask about both. Every capability claim that does appear in these pages is tied to a named Microsoft documentation page and the date it was verified, so you can check whether the claim still holds on the day you read it. Everything that moves quarterly, console procedures, plan tiers, preview statuses, configuration walkthroughs, lives in the book's companion annex, maintained against current documentation at sougataroy.com/who-owns-the-agent-annex. When a chapter says fast-decaying detail lives in the companion annex, this page is what it means. The same division of labor sets this book's edition plan:

this first edition reflects the platform as verified through August 2026, a second edition is planned for 2028, and the questions in print are expected to outlive both.

One implication belongs at the front rather than waiting to be discovered at Chapter 14. The details will have moved by the time this page is in your hands. The questions will not have. If a screen described here has been renamed, the thing to check is not whether the book is out of date. It is whether your answer to the question the screen was illustrating exists yet.

# A VOCABULARY OF ACCOUNTABILITY

**Every term below answers a question someone will eventually be asked to answer out loud. The definitions are here so that the answer is available before the question arrives.**

---

## AGENT AUTHORIZATION

**What it is.** A decision, made before an agent operates, by a named person with the standing to make it, that this identified agent may act for a stated purpose within defined permissions, prohibitions, and review conditions.

**What it is not.** Not an identity, not a license, not a connector consent, not a deployment. Each of those is something the organization did. This is something the organization decided.

**The evidence it produces.** A dated record bound to the agent's stable technical identifier, signed before the agent went to production.

**Who is accountable.** The approving authority for the decision itself, with the business owner and the technical operator accountable only for the parts of the record assigned to them by name.

**The examination question it answers.** What decision allowed this agent to begin operating, and who had the authority to make it?

---

## THE AUTHORIZATION LAYER

**What it is.** The set of organizational decisions that has to exist beneath the platform controls, establishing who decided that the agent may operate, the limits of that operation, and the authority behind the decision.

**What it is not.** Not a product, not a console, and not a technical control. A vendor can provide the controls and the settings. The organization still has to make the decisions that give those controls their purpose.

**The evidence it produces.** A dated and signed record that names a person, defines the agent's scope, and identifies the conditions that require the authorization to be reconsidered.

**Who is accountable.** The business authority with the standing to accept the risk, separate from the team that built or administers the agent.

**The examination question it answers.** Who authorized this agent, and can you show me the decision behind that authorization rather than the configuration?

---

## THE AUTHORIZATION RECORD

**What it is.** The single artifact that carries an agent's purpose, permitted actions, explicit prohibitions, data scope, accountable people, review triggers, and a signature that predates production.
**What it is not.** Not a change ticket, not an intake form, and not a deployment approval. Those record that something was done. This records that someone accepted it.
**The evidence it produces.** Itself. An undated one is worth nothing as evidence of prior authorization.
**Who is accountable.** The named signer, until the authorization is renewed, narrowed, or withdrawn. A successor acquires the role by transfer and the accountability only by signing again.
**The examination question it answers.** Show me the record of a named human being who understood this scope, weighed it, and accepted it before the agent went to production.

---

## THE ACCOUNTABILITY ASSUMPTION

**What it is.** The condition in which every function believes another function owns an agent's risk, and the belief is unanimous, reciprocal, and unwritten.
**What it is not.** Not negligence, and not a gap in the org chart. Every party is behaving reasonably; the failure is that reasonable behavior does not intersect anywhere.
**The evidence it produces.** None, and that absence is the diagnostic. The assumption is visible only as a missing record.

**Who is accountable.** The organization, without exception. Internally, no named person has accepted it, and that absence is the finding.
**The examination question it answers.** When four teams each name a different owner, which answer does the organization stand behind?

---

## INTENT ARCHITECTURE

**What it is.** The practice of writing down what an agent is for, and what it may not do, before it is capable of doing anything.
**What it is not.** Not prompt engineering and not system instructions. Those tell a model how to behave. This tells the organization what it has agreed to.
**The evidence it produces.** A purpose statement and a prohibition list that were authored before deployment and can be shown to predate it.
**Who is accountable.** The business owner who defined the purpose, jointly with whoever approved the prohibitions.
**The examination question it answers.** What was this agent supposed to do, according to a document written before it did anything?

---

## THE CHAIN AUTHORIZATION GAP

**What it is.** The condition in which each agent in a multi-agent chain is individually approved, no one approved the chain, and the original approval travels the whole length unrevisited.

### Who Owns the Agent?

**What it is not.** Not a permissions failure. Every hop is permitted. The aggregate authority is what no one granted.
**The evidence it produces.** A chain-level record produced before the chain runs, answering origin, authority, delegation, and effect boundary, with the trigger list that reopens it.
**Who is accountable.** The authority over the business process the chain executes, not the owner of any single agent in it.
**The examination question it answers.** Who approved what these agents can do together, as opposed to separately?

---

## TENANT AGENT RECONCILIATION

**What it is.** The periodic exercise of comparing every agent the platform can see against every agent the organization has authorized, and assigning a disposition to each difference.
**What it is not.** Not an inventory. An inventory counts. Reconciliation compares two counts and forces a decision about each discrepancy.
**The evidence it produces.** A dated reconciliation report with a named disposition for every unmatched agent.
**Who is accountable.** The function that holds the authorization register, which must not be the function that operates the platform.
**The examination question it answers.** How many agents are running, how many did you authorize, and what did you do about the difference?

---

## THE AUTHORIZATION COVERAGE LIFECYCLE

**What it is.** The path an organization travels from not knowing what it runs, to knowing, to preventing new unauthorized deployment faster than it accumulates.

**What it is not.** Not a maturity score and not a certification. It describes a condition, and organizations move backward through it without noticing.

**The evidence it produces.** A ratio: authorized agents over discovered agents, measured on a date, trending.

**Who is accountable.** Whoever owns the intake gate, because that is where the direction of travel is decided.

**The examination question it answers.** Is your authorized population growing faster or slower than your actual population?

---

## THE DISPOSITION PROTOCOL

**What it is.** The standing rule that every signal about an agent, whether a change, a failure, a departure, or a platform announcement, receives a recorded decision rather than a reaction.

**What it is not.** Not incident response and not change management. Those handle events. This handles the question of whether an authorization still holds after the event.

**The evidence it produces.** A disposition entry per signal: renewed, narrowed, suspended, retired, or accepted as-is, with a date and a name.

**Who is accountable.** The original signer where they remain in role, and an explicitly named successor where they do not.

**The examination question it answers.** This changed in March. Who decided the approval still stood, and when?

---

## AGENT SPRAWL

*A shared industry term. What this book adds is its measurement against an authorization register rather than only against an inventory.*

**What it is.** The accumulation of agents faster than any function can account for them.

**What it is not.** Not shadow IT renamed. Most sprawl is sanctioned, licensed, and visible. It is unauthorized, not unknown.

**The evidence it produces.** The gap between the platform's count and the register's count.

**Who is accountable.** Whoever permitted creation without an intake step, which is usually no one in particular.

**The examination question it answers.** Of the agents running today, how many entered through a gate?

---

## THE INTENT GAP

*A shared industry term. What this book adds is its application to agent authorization, where the gap sits between what was approved and what the agent now does.*

**What it is.** The distance between what a system was intended to do and what it actually does.

**What it is not.** Not model drift. The model may be unchanged. The gap opens because the environment, the data, or the use moved underneath a frozen decision.

**The evidence it produces.** A comparison of current behavior against the purpose statement in the authorization record.

**Who is accountable.** The reviewer named in the record, whose job is to notice that the two no longer match.

**The examination question it answers.** Does this agent still do what the approval said it would do?

---

# PART 1: THE QUESTION

An examiner is about to ask your organization seven questions, and these first three chapters are about why the honest answer to most of them is silence. Chapter 1 stages the examination. Chapter 2 traces how accountability for AI agents gets assumed instead of assigned, by everyone, about someone else. Chapter 3 walks Microsoft's own governance tooling against the seven questions and marks where the platform's answers stop.

# Chapter 1

# The Examiner Walks In

The advisory arrived on a Tuesday.

It carried the identifier CW1226324, one entry among dozens in the Microsoft 365 admin center's service health feed that week, formatted like every routine service notice your tenant administrators have learned to skim. This one was not routine. In February 2026, Microsoft acknowledged that Copilot Chat had incorrectly processed some customer email messages, including content carrying sensitivity labels and content subject to data loss prevention policies.

Read that sentence the way a compliance officer read it that morning. The labels were the control. The DLP policy was the control. For a period before the fix, Copilot had processed some of the protected mail anyway.

Microsoft's advisory was careful, and the care mattered. Access controls remained intact, the company said. The bug had caused Copilot to behave "contrary to its intended protection model," not to bypass the underlying authorization. In plain language: nobody saw mail they lacked permission to see, but the software that was supposed to respect the labels had not respected them.

For the engineers, that distinction settled things. A bug was found, a fix was shipped, the protection model was restored. For everyone else in the building, the distinction settled nothing at all, because the question that surfaced in the meetings that followed was not a question about the bug.

Picture that meeting in any organization where Copilot Chat was live that month. A conference room, a projected copy of the advisory, a general counsel, a CISO, someone from records management who was invited late. The advisory gets read aloud. Someone asks how many mailboxes were in scope. Someone asks whether notification obligations attach. And then someone asks the question that changes the temperature of the room.

Who approved Copilot reading labeled mail in the first place?

Not who configured it. Configuration has an answer; there is an admin, a change ticket, a date. Who approved it. Which human being in this organization looked at the scenario, an AI system processing every employee's email including the labeled and policy-protected portions, accepted the risk of that scenario on the organization's behalf, and signed something.

In some organizations, that question had an answer. A document existed. It named the scenario, defined what the system was permitted to touch, recorded the exclusions, and carried the signature of a person who was still employed there and knew they had signed it. When the advisory arrived, those organizations pulled the document, compared the incident to the authorized scope, and had a position they could state to a board or a regulator before any investigation began. The position might have been uncomfortable. It existed.

In most organizations, the question produced silence, then archaeology. Someone found the deployment ticket. Someone found the licensing decision, which was a procurement event, not a risk acceptance. Someone found the rollout communications, which announced the tool but authorized nothing. The organization discovered, in real time and in front of its own lawyers, that its entire governance artifact for an AI system reading corporate email was the way the tool had been set up.

A configuration is a description of settings. It is not a decision, it names no one, and it accepts nothing. When the tool behaves exactly as configured, nobody notices the difference. The difference only becomes visible on the day the tool does something else, which is precisely the day you need the document you do not have.

The bug was patched within weeks. The question it exposed has no patch.

## The request list

Now move the scene eighteen months forward and make it formal. The person asking is no longer your general counsel. She is an examiner, from your banking regulator or your insurance commissioner or your health system's auditor, and she has sent the document request in advance, the way examiners do, so that the meeting is not a discussion but a production.

In January 2026, FINRA published "Emerging Trend in GenAI: Observations on AI Agents," documenting what its staff was already seeing inside member firms: AI agents acting across systems, and examination questions forming around who authorized them and what records covered their actions. When a regulator publishes observations, it is telling you what the request list will contain. The questions below are not FINRA's. They are the ones those observations lead to, in the order an examination is likely to proceed: population first, then the individual record, then the hard cases, then currency.

**How many AI agents are operating in your environment right now, and how does that number compare to the number your organization approved?**

**For this agent: who authorized it, and what exactly was it authorized to do?**

**When it acts outside that scope, which named human answers? Not a team. A name.**

**This outcome came from multiple agents acting in sequence. Whose authorization covers the chain?**

**Your systems of record show the change the agent made. Can they show who sanctioned it?**

**Your monitoring flagged this before the incident. What were you required to do when the flag fired, and did you do it?**

**Is any of this current? When was this authorization last revisited, and what change would have forced a revisit?**

Two of the seven, the chain question and the monitoring question, do not yet have an incident behind them in this chapter. They will get theirs.

Sit with the first one for a moment, because it is the one organizations fail before the examination even reaches an agent. The examiner is not asking for your intentions. She is asking for two numbers and the gap between them: the count of agents your directory can see, and the count your governance process approved. In most enterprises those two numbers have never been placed in the same document, and the people who could produce each number have never met.

In practice the request arrives narrower and harsher than the list above. Produce the authorization record, the named owner, and the last review evidence for the five most active agents in the last quarter. Sampling is how examiners work, and the sample is how they decide whether to widen.

Now the second and third. Notice what they are not asking. They are not asking whether the agent has an identity; Microsoft Entra Agent ID exists to give it one, and the examiner knows that. They are not asking for logs; Microsoft Purview can capture Copilot and agent interactions in the unified audit log, and the examiner knows that too. Identity proves the agent exists. Logs prove what it did. The questions ask for something neither artifact contains: proof of what it was permitted to do, and the name of the person who granted the permission.

*The platform can prove what the agent did. Only you can prove what it was allowed to do.*

That sentence is the book. Everything that follows is the architecture that makes it answerable, but the gap it describes is worth stating in its rawest form now. Your Microsoft tenant can generate an extensive record of agent activity: prompts, responses, files touched, sensitivity labels encountered, handoffs timestamped where the service supports it. When the examiner arrives, you will be able to reconstruct most of what the agent did.

What you will not be able to produce, unless someone built it, is a single page stating that the agent was authorized to do those things, by a named person, on a recorded date, within a defined scope. An extensive record of activity is not a partial record of authority. It is a record of nothing the examiner asked for.

Every organization already understands this distinction perfectly. It just applies it to a different species.

The examiner asks | What she needs | The usual answer | The framework

**Seven questions, and what each one is really asking for**

| The examiner asks | What she needs | The usual answer | The framework |
|---|---|---|---|
| How many agents are operating, and how many were approved? | Two numbers, and the gap between them | One number, from whichever system was asked | Tenant Agent Reconciliation |
| Who authorized this agent, and to do what? | A signed record predating deployment | A ticket showing a capability was enabled | The Agent Authorization Record |
| When it acts outside scope, which named human answers? | A name | A team, or a role that turns out to be vacant | The Accountability Assumption |
| This outcome came from agents in sequence. Whose authorization covers the chain? | One record covering the composition | Several records, each covering a part | The Chain Authorization Gap |
| Your systems show the change. Can they show who sanctioned it? | The authorization, not the action | The action, in detail | Intent Architecture |
| Monitoring flagged this. What were you required to do? | A written obligation with a clock on it | An alert, and a recollection of who saw it | The Disposition Protocol |
| Is any of this current? | A review date and a trigger list | The original approval, undated since | Authorization Coverage Lifecycle |

*The examination proceeds in this order because it is the order in which answers get harder. Most organizations fail the first question, before an examiner has looked at a single agent.*

## The matrix you already have

Somewhere in your organization there is a delegation of authority matrix. It may be called a signature authority policy, or a DOA, or Appendix C of the finance manual. It states, in a table nobody finds remarkable, that a manager may approve expenses to ten thousand dollars, a vice president to one hundred thousand, and that anything above five million requires the board. It has rules for sub-delegation. It has rules for what happens when the approver is on leave. It is versioned, and internal audit checks transactions against it every year.

Nobody defends this document, because nobody attacks it. It is simply understood that in an organization of any size, the authority to commit the organization must be explicit, bounded, personal, and written down before it is exercised. An employee who wired two million dollars and then explained that no policy specifically prohibited it would not keep the explanation or the job.

Then the organization deployed agents, and the entire discipline evaporated.

The agent that summarizes contracts, drafts customer responses, moves records between systems, and triggers downstream workflows arrived with no line in any matrix. An agent that sends a customer-facing email, updates a CRM record, or starts a payment workflow is exercising delegated authority in the plainest sense; the policy manual has simply never described it that way. It commits the organization dozens of times an hour. Its spending limit, if the concept were applied, is undefined, which in a delegation framework does not mean zero. It means unlimited, pending the incident that forces the question.

The comparison is not rhetorical. It is the examiner's actual frame of reference, because delegation of authority is the governance discipline examiners were trained on before AI existed. When she asks who authorized the agent, she is asking the same question she would ask about a wire transfer, and she expects the same species of answer: a name, a scope, a date, a document. The organization that answers "the platform logs everything" has responded to a delegation question with a surveillance answer. The examiner will write that down, and not in the way you hope.

## The floor

If any doubt remains about whether the organization owns the agent's actions, a tribunal in British Columbia removed it two years before the advisory arrived.

In late 2022, a man named Jake Moffatt needed to fly for his grandmother's funeral. Air Canada's website chatbot told him he could book at full fare and apply for the bereavement discount afterward. The airline's actual policy said no such thing; bereavement fares could not be claimed retroactively. Moffatt booked on the chatbot's word, applied for the refund, and was denied, because the chatbot had been wrong about the company's own policy.

The dispute reached the British Columbia Civil Resolution Tribunal, and Air Canada made an argument that will be quoted in governance decks for a decade. The airline submitted that it could not be held liable for information provided by its "agents, servants, or representatives," a category in which it included the chatbot. The chatbot, in effect, was responsible for its own statements.

The tribunal's decision, Moffatt v. Air Canada, 2024 BCCRT 149, issued on February 14, 2024, rejected the argument in a single dry phrase, calling it "a remarkable submission." The chatbot was part of Air Canada's website, the company was responsible for all the information on its website, and customers were under no obligation to cross-check one part of the site against another. Air Canada paid $812.02 in damages, interest, and fees.

The number is the point, and the point is not the number. Eight hundred dollars is less than Air Canada's legal team spent discussing it. What the ruling established is the floor under everything in this book: the separate-entity argument was available, a well-resourced airline made it in writing, and it did not survive contact with a tribunal. The organization owns the agent's behavior the way it owns its published prices and its signed contracts. When the agent speaks, the organization has spoken. When the agent acts, the organization has acted.

Notice what the ruling did not do. It assigned accountability after the fact, to the organization as a whole, through litigation. It said nothing about how accountability should be designed inside the organization before the incident, because that is not a tribunal's job. Nothing in the ruling tells you which of your executives should have signed for the chatbot, what the signature should have covered, or how the authorization should have been revisited when the bot's knowledge sources changed. The law can establish, after the fact, that you own the outcome. The architecture of owning it in advance, on paper, with names, is left entirely to you.

That silence is the space this book occupies.

## What the answer looks like

Return to the two organizations from the advisory morning, because the difference between them is now precise enough to state.

Both ran the same Microsoft stack. Both had the same licenses, the same Purview audit trail, the same Entra identities, the same advisory in the same service health feed. The technical posture was identical. What differed was a document: one organization possessed a written record, produced before deployment, stating what the AI scenario was, what it was authorized to touch, what it was forbidden to touch, and which named person had accepted the scenario on the organization's behalf. The other possessed a configuration.

The document did not prevent the bug. Nothing the organization wrote could have; the bug was Microsoft's. What the document changed was every hour that followed. The first organization could distinguish, immediately and in writing, between the scenario it had authorized and the behavior the advisory described, which converted an ambient panic into a bounded incident with a defined owner. The second organization could not say what had gone wrong, because it had never said what going right was supposed to look like.

This book exists to move organizations from the second position to the first, on the Microsoft stack specifically, because that is where the agents are. Microsoft 365 Copilot reaches employees in days. Copilot Studio agents launch in hours. Power Platform automations cross system boundaries before anyone with the word "risk" in their title hears about them. Agent 365, generally available since May 2026, offers a control plane to discover, observe, and govern agents across Microsoft 365 and supported integrations. The deployment is fast because Microsoft made it fast. Microsoft did not make the accountability, because accountability is not a product. No vendor can sell you a decision that only your organization can make.

What the chapters ahead provide is the architecture of that decision. A way of designing intent before deployment, so that the agent's scope is a choice rather than a discovery. A document that turns the choice into evidence: names, scope, exclusions, date, signature. And an operating model that keeps the evidence alive, because an authorization that was true at launch and never revisited is not a living record. It is launch paperwork, and examiners have a specific question for launch paperwork.

The seven questions above will return at the end of this book, asked by the same examiner, in the same order. By then, every one of them will have an answer that can be produced from a record rather than assembled from archaeology. That is the entire distance the book travels: from the silence in the conference room to a folder that opens.

Before turning the page, run the smallest version of the examination yourself. Take the most active agent in your tenant, the one that touched the most mail or moved the most records this week. Your admin center can probably name it faster than your governance process can. Now name the human being who signed for it. Not the person who built it, not the team that operates it, not the executive who would probably be blamed. The person who authorized it, in writing, before it ran.

If a name came to mind, the next nineteen chapters will test whether the paper behind that name would survive the request list. If no name came to mind, you have just met the gap this book is about, and it is worth noticing that the agent did not stop working while you were thinking. It is running right now, under an authority no one can produce, and the only reason that feels normal is that no one has asked yet.

Chapter 2

# The Accountability Assumption in Microsoft Environments

Fifty-one.

That was the number chief information officers gave when Cisco asked, between 2013 and 2015, how many cloud services were running in their enterprises. The answers were not careless. The executives giving them had procurement records, approved vendor lists, and security review queues, and the number fifty-one came out of those artifacts. It was an honest count of the part of the enterprise that asks permission.

Then Cisco measured. Its Cloud Consumption Service, a practice founded by Bob Dimicco, analyzed actual production network traffic at large enterprises across the United States, Europe, Canada, and Australia from January 2013 through July 2015. The traffic showed an average of 730 cloud services in use per enterprise.

Not fifty-one with rounding error. Fourteen times fifty-one. Regulated industries did worse, not better: healthcare and financial services organizations were running seventeen to twenty times more services than their IT departments estimated. By January 2016, Cisco's follow-up measurement put the large-enterprise average at 1,220 services against an IT estimate of 91.

Hold the gap in view for a moment, because the gap is the subject of this chapter. Six hundred seventy-nine services, on average, that existed in production traffic and nowhere in the official count. Nobody smuggled them in. Marketing signed up for an analytics tool because marketing needed analytics. A project team adopted a file-sharing service because the deadline was Thursday. Every one of those adoptions was made by a person solving a real problem, and every one carried a small, silent belief along with it: someone else is tracking this. It runs on the corporate network, so IT must see it. Someone approved the expense, so procurement must have a record. The tool asked for my work credentials, so security must have vetted it.

The CIOs, meanwhile, believed their number because it came from a process, and the process was real. Requests were reviewed. Vendors were assessed. The fifty-one was not a lie. It was a complete inventory of the things people had asked about.

Ten years later, the question has changed by one word. Ask a technology leader today how many AI agents operate in the company's Microsoft tenant, and the answer will come from the same place the fifty-one came from: the approved list, the intake queue, the projects governance heard about. The measurement side has changed too, because Microsoft Entra can now enumerate agent identities in the directory, which means the honest count is a few clicks away in a way the 2015 traffic analysis never was. The two numbers will not match, for the same reason they did not match in 2015. But one thing about the repeat is new, and it is not a detail. An unaccounted cloud service holds data. An unaccounted agent acts. It sends the email, updates the record, and starts the workflow, under an identity, at whatever speed it was built to run.

The counting problem has a name and a chapter of its own. This chapter is about the belief that produces the gap. Six hundred seventy-nine services did not accumulate because hundreds of employees decided to evade governance. They accumulated because hundreds of employees, and their CIO, were all operating under the same assumption at the same time, each certain that accountability lived somewhere specific, and each pointing at a different somewhere. To see how that works with agents, watch it happen to four reasonable people.

## Four reasonable people

Picture a regional insurer, a claims operation of a few hundred adjusters, and a senior business analyst who is good at her job. Adjusters keep interrupting each other to ask about claim status, so she builds an agent in Copilot Studio that answers those questions directly, reading from the claims tracking list and the policy library on SharePoint. It takes her part of an afternoon. When the agent needs to connect to the data, a consent dialog appears on her screen listing the permissions; she reads it, it matches what she is trying to do, she clicks accept with her own credentials. The agent works. Adjusters love it. There is no ticket anywhere in the enterprise with this agent's name on it, because at no point did any screen ask her to file one.

Six weeks later, a compliance analyst preparing evidence for a state market-conduct examination finds the agent while sampling systems that touch claims data, and asks the question this book turns on. Who approved this?

Ask the builder first. Her answer is not evasive, and it is worth hearing in full, because it is correct at every step. The company licensed Copilot Studio. IT decides which connectors are even available in her environment; whole categories are blocked. The consent screen showed her exactly what the agent would access, and she consented. Everything she did, the platform permitted her to do, on a system her employer bought and configured for exactly this kind of building. In her understanding, the license was the approval.

Ask the platform administrator next. He can pull up the Power Platform admin center and show you the environment, the data loss prevention policies he maintains, the connector groupings he curates. His domain is capacity, policy boundaries, and tenant hygiene. The environment contains several hundred makers. He does not review what they make, because reviewing use cases has never been his job, and no version of his job description would survive it becoming his job. The business owns the use case.

Ask the builder's vice president. She encouraged the pilot; it visibly saved adjuster time, and she said so in a staff meeting. Her operating belief is simple and widely shared: anything running on the corporate platform passed security review before the platform was offered to her team. Security reviewed the tool, therefore security stands behind what the tool builds.

Ask security last. This is the first they have heard of it. They did review Copilot Studio, as a product, in a vendor and platform assessment before the licensing decision. They did not review this agent, because no intake ever existed for this agent, and their review process, like every review process, begins with being asked.

Four people. Four answers, each locally reasonable, each pointing at another chair. The builder points at the platform team. The platform team points at the business. The business points at security. Security points at an intake queue that was never used. Stack the four beliefs and they form a circle, and the circle encloses nothing. The agent was approved by the sum of four people's confidence in each other's paperwork.

Notice what is absent from this story: malice, negligence, even carelessness. Everyone did their job as their job was defined. The failure is not in any of the four chairs. It sits in the space between them, and spaces between chairs do not appear on org charts, which is why nobody is assigned to watch them.

## The assumption goes to court

For anyone tempted to file this under hypothetical, the same circle is currently being litigated in federal court, at scale, with the pointing happening under oath.

Mobley v. Workday, Inc. was filed on February 21, 2023, in the Northern District of California, before Judge Rita F. Lin. The plaintiffs allege that Workday's AI-based applicant screening tools discriminated against job seekers by race, age, and disability before any human ever reviewed them. Workday's litigation position is the vendor's side of the circle: it provides technology, and its customers make the hiring decisions. The operating posture of many customers over the same years was the mirror image: the platform handled the screening, so the platform handled the screening's consequences. The two beliefs cannot both be true. In July 2024, the court declined to let Workday's version end the case, allowing claims to proceed on the theory that Workday plausibly acted as an agent of the employers using it. On May 16, 2025, the court granted preliminary certification of a collective action, and on February 17, 2026, it authorized notice to every person aged forty or older who applied for a job through Workday's platform since September 24, 2020. As of mid-2026 the case is deep in discovery, with the parties fighting over bias-testing data and privilege in orders running into the hundreds of docket entries.

Nothing in the public record shows a pre-deployment document, on either side, resolving who owned the screening outcomes before the screening ran. That resolution is happening now instead, through motions and discovery orders, years after deployment, at litigation prices, while thousands of employers who received the case's opt-in notices learn what their assumption was worth. The four interviews at the insurer and the docket in San Francisco are the same structure at different altitudes. Everyone assumed. A court now decides.

## The populated field

Here the Microsoft stack enters, and it enters, at first glance, as the solution.

Open the Microsoft Entra admin center in a tenant running agents and look at what the directory now contains. The directory now has a place for this. Agents are first-class objects in Entra, with their own schema (Microsoft Learn, verified July 4, 2026). Better still, the schema distinguishes roles that most organizations have never distinguished on paper: an agent identity carries owners, who administer it, and a sponsor, the role Microsoft's documentation defines as recording "the human user or group that's accountable" for the agent, with sponsors holding the business accountability for its purpose and its lifecycle decisions (Microsoft Learn, learn.microsoft.com/entra/agent-id/agent-identities, verified August 13, 2026). Read that definition twice. Microsoft has encoded, in the directory schema, the exact distinction between running an agent and answering for it that the four interviews could not produce. This is the schema a thoughtful examiner would have designed.

Now watch it get populated. When the analyst at the insurer published her claims agent, Copilot Studio automatically registered an agent identity in the Entra tenant, with her recorded as sponsor (Microsoft Learn, verified July 4, 2026). No step was skipped, because no step was presented to skip. The compliance analyst who later found the agent found it through exactly this record, and the record was genuinely useful: a name, a creation date, an object to investigate. Every fact in the directory was true.

And every reader of that directory drew the same conclusion the four interviews produced, with more confidence, because now there was a field. A populated sponsor attribute looks like an answered question. Whoever browses the tenant sees an agent with a named accountable human and reasonably infers that sponsorship was considered, offered, and accepted, the way it would be for any accountable role a person holds. What actually happened is that a default fired. The field records who clicked publish. The inference records a governance event that never occurred.

Microsoft has since gone further, and the further step deserves an honest reading. Entra now documents owner, sponsor, and manager as distinct administrative relationships for agent identities, and ships sponsor lifecycle workflows that automate sponsor maintenance and reassignment when the named human leaves or changes roles (Microsoft Learn, verified July 9, 2026). This solves a real problem. Orphaned agents, running for years under the identity of someone who departed, are among the ugliest artifacts in any tenant, and machinery that keeps the sponsor field current is machinery examiners will eventually expect. But notice what the workflow does. When a sponsor leaves, it names a successor. The directory is never stale, the field is never empty, and at no point in the process does the newly named human accept anything. Accountability transfers as a directory operation, completed in less time than it takes the new sponsor to read the notification, assuming the notification is read at all.

That is the assumption from the previous sections, executed at machine speed. The four reasonable people each believed accountability lived with someone else; the workflow now writes down who that someone is, keeps the entry fresh, and asks no one. None of this is a flaw in the schema. The fields do what fields do: they record facts of administration. What an examiner will ask for is a fact of a different kind, an act rather than an attribute, a human who accepted this agent's risks in writing before it ran. A directory cannot contain that, no matter how well maintained, and the better maintained it is, the fewer people will ever think to ask whether the acceptance behind the field exists.

## One agent, three departments

Assumptions of this kind are cheap right up until an agent does something that costs money, so construct the day one does. The scenario is assembled, not reported, but every component in it ships today.

A business analyst in customer operations builds a retention agent. It identifies accounts at risk of leaving, using churn scores that live in the CRM, which sales operations owns. It checks payment and fee history to shape an offer, reading tables that finance owns. It reads recent support tickets for sentiment, data that customer service owns. It drafts the outreach email and sends it through a shared mailbox, using a service connection, so even the identity doing the sending belongs to no individual person. Every connection was consented to through a dialog. Every permission was technically grantable, so every permission was granted.

One Tuesday, the agent includes a late-fee waiver in retention offers sent to 214 delinquent accounts, a category finance had explicitly excluded from waivers in a policy memo the agent never read, because nobody had connected the memo to anything the agent could reach. Customers accept the offers. The company honors them, because the alternative is telling 214 customers the email from the company was not from the company, and Chapter 1 covered how that argument fares. The cost is real but survivable. The incident review is where the actual damage surfaces.

Walk the room. The builder followed the data she could reach; nothing she touched was forbidden to her. Sales operations owns the churn model, not what anyone does with its scores. Finance owns the fee policy and is learning today that an agent has been reading its tables for months. Customer service owns the mailbox the offers came from and nothing else. The platform administrator owns the environment, not the use case; he has said this sentence before. Security has no finding to write, because the agent did exactly what it was configured to do, and there is no incident category for that. Six functions are present, each with clean hands, and the meeting cannot answer its own first agenda item, which is whose incident this is.

Every employee in that room has a manager of record. If any one of them had personally waived those fees, accountability would resolve in a single hop up the org chart, before the meeting was even scheduled, because that is what org charts are for: every person in the enterprise sits inside exactly one box, with a name above it. The agent that waived the fees has an owner field, a sponsor field, a service connection, and not one person at the table who would say "that's mine" without a qualifier attached. The incident review was the best-attended meeting of the agent's life. Its deployment had no meeting at all.

## The name for it

The pattern now has enough evidence behind it to be named. The Accountability Assumption is the implicit belief that accountability for an AI system's behavior resides with whoever built it, licensed it, hosts it, or profits from it. With someone, in every case, provided the someone is someone else. It is not a position anyone argues for, which is why it is never argued against. Nobody at the insurer decided that the claims agent would run unowned, and nobody deploying Workday decided that screening outcomes belonged to no one. The assumption is not a decision. It is what fills the space where a decision was supposed to happen, and it fills that space so smoothly that from every seat in the chain, it looks like diligence.

It wears three costumes, all of which have now appeared in this chapter. The vendor will handle it: Workday's customers, learning otherwise by court-authorized notice. The platform will handle it: everyone who read a populated sponsor field as an answered question. Someone internal will handle it: four reasonable people, arranged in a circle. Different costumes, same anatomy. Every approval anyone can point to is an approval for something to exist, a license, an environment, a connector policy. No approval anywhere covers the outcomes the agent produces. The assumption is what stands in the gap between those two kinds of approval, holding the weight that a signature was supposed to hold.

Closing it takes less machinery than most organizations fear and more nerve than most expect. The closure is a person: a named individual on the business side who accepts, in writing, before the agent enters production, accountability for what the agent does, and who could explain to an examiner why the agent should exist without consulting its configuration. Not the builder, who made it work. Not the administrator, who keeps it running. Not the vendor, whose contract has been disclaiming this exact liability all along, in language that was never hidden from anyone who read it. A named human, an accepted scope, a date that precedes the first live action. Later chapters give that record a full anatomy. Its existence is the entire difference between an organization that assigned accountability and an organization that assumed it.

Accountability was never assigned. It was assumed, by everyone, about someone else.

The test costs nothing and can be run this week. Pick one agent in your tenant, ideally one that touches money or customers, and conduct the four interviews yourself, in order: the person who built it, the team that administers the platform, the executive who benefits from it, the security function that would answer for it in an examination. You will get four confident answers. If any two of them point at each other, you have found the circle, and it has been running your agent since the day it went live. The uncomfortable part is not the finding. The uncomfortable part is that the interviews take an afternoon, they have been available to you the whole time, and the only people who reliably conduct them are examiners and plaintiffs' counsel, and when they conduct them, the interviews are called depositions.

## What each party believes someone else has done

| The party | What they believe | What they actually did | What nobody did |
|---|---|---|---|
| The platform vendor | The customer configures and governs their own tenant | Shipped a capability with defaults | Decide what this specific agent may do |
| The deploying team | Governance approved the platform | Built inside an approved platform | Authorize this agent's scope |
| The approver | The technical team validated it | Signed a request describing a capability | Name what the agent is prohibited from doing |
| The examiner | Someone holds the record | Asked for it | Nothing. She is the one asking. |

*The assumption is not that governance happened. It is that governance happened elsewhere, performed by someone whose name nobody can produce.*

## Chapter 3

# Why Microsoft Defaults Don't Answer Who Owns the Agent

Somewhere in your tenant, within the last hour, a record like this one was written.

It lives in the Microsoft Purview unified audit log, one row among the thousands generated that day. Expanded on a compliance analyst's screen, it shows an operation identifying a Copilot interaction. A timestamp in UTC, to the second. The account the interaction ran under. References to the resources touched: three files on a SharePoint site, each listed by location, each carrying its sensitivity label, one of them marked Confidential. The prompt and the response are preserved as well, stored in the user's mailbox, which means they are subject to eDiscovery and legal hold like any other mail, and the transcript is retrievable through Purview's data security posture management tooling for AI (Microsoft Learn,
learn.microsoft.com/en-us/purview/audit-copilot and

learn.microsoft.com/en-us/purview/ai-m365-copilot, verified August 13, 2026).

Read the record the way it was built to be read, as an evidence exhibit. It establishes what happened with a completeness almost nothing else in your enterprise can match. Which identity acted. When, to the second. What it read, what it produced, which protected content it encountered along the way. An employee who spent the same ten minutes at the same files would leave a thinner trail. The most thoroughly documented ten minutes of work in your organization today almost certainly belong to software.

Now ask the record the question this book turns on. Was any of this allowed?

Be precise about what the question means, because the record contains a decoy answer. Every access in that row succeeded, and it succeeded because the identity held permission to the files it touched. Permission was checked, in real time, by systems that do that job well. But permission is a property of a credential. It tells you what the account could reach. The question an examiner asks is one layer up: who decided it should? Which human being looked at this scenario, an AI system reading labeled files and generating output from them, and accepted it, in advance, on the organization's behalf?

Scroll the record top to bottom. There is no field for that. Not because Microsoft's engineers forgot a column. A log captures events, and in most organizations the authorization of this agent was never an event. Nothing occurred that any system, from any vendor, at any price, could have recorded. The log is a perfect witness to everything that happened. Authorization is the one thing in this story that didn't.

That absence is the subject of this chapter, and it needs careful handling, because the easy version of the argument is wrong. The easy version says Microsoft under-built governance. The truthful version is stranger and more useful: Microsoft has built more governance machinery for agents, faster, than any platform vendor in the industry, and the machinery is genuinely good, and the question still comes back empty. Understanding why requires taking honest inventory of what the machinery does. So take it.

## What Microsoft actually ships

Start with identity, because Microsoft started there. Agent identities are now a distinct object type in Microsoft Entra, modeled as service principals with an agent subtype; the directory's object model includes agent identities, agent identity blueprints, and agent users as first-class citizens (Microsoft Learn, verified July 4, 2026). This matters more than it sounds. For years, automation hid inside service accounts and borrowed credentials, indistinguishable in the directory from a backup job. An agent in a current Microsoft tenant can now exist as itself: enumerable, filterable, a thing the directory admits is a thing. Microsoft Entra Agent ID provides the platform for creating and managing these identities, and its capabilities are included for agents managed through Agent 365, which has been generally available since May 1, 2026 (Microsoft Learn what's-new documentation, verified July 9, 2026).

The schema goes further, into territory most enterprises have never formalized on paper. An agent identity carries owners, who administer it, and a sponsor, the human accountable for the agent's purpose and its lifecycle decisions, with owner, sponsor, and manager documented as distinct administrative relationships (Microsoft Learn, verified July 4 and July 9, 2026). Chapter 2 spent time with the sponsor field and what a populated one does to the humans who read it. Here, credit the design on its own terms: the schema distinguishes running an agent from answering for one, which is a distinction plenty of governance committees have failed to draw with a whiteboard and an afternoon. Microsoft even ships lifecycle workflows that keep the sponsor field current when the named human leaves or changes roles (Microsoft Learn, verified July 9, 2026). The directory, at least, will never shrug.

Activity capture is broader still. Beyond the unified audit log entry that opened this chapter, Copilot Studio agent interactions flow into Purview, with transcripts surfaced through DSPM for AI; Microsoft applications including Copilot Studio and Microsoft Foundry apps are covered under standard audit licensing, while non-Microsoft AI applications can be logged on a pay-as-you-go basis with 180-day retention; and for agents holding Microsoft Entra Agent IDs, authentication activity lands in the Entra sign-in logs as well (Microsoft Learn, learn.microsoft.com/en-us/microsoft-copilot-studio/admin-logging-copilot-studio, verified August 13, 2026). The Copilot Control System organizes the administrative surface on top, with its governance documentation splitting controls by license tier, foundational at E3 and optimized at E5 (Microsoft Learn, learn.microsoft.com/en-us/microsoft-365/copilot/copilot-control-system/security-governance, verified August 13, 2026).

Then, in April 2026, Microsoft did something that surprised people who track this space. It open-sourced a runtime enforcement layer. The Agent Governance Toolkit, released April 2, 2026 under the MIT license, is a policy engine that intercepts an agent's actions before execution and evaluates each one against declarative rules, shipping as SDKs for Python, TypeScript, .NET, Rust, and Go (Microsoft Open Source Blog, April 2, 2026, verified August 13, 2026). A policy can block a destructive operation or route an action to a human approver before it fires. This is real governance machinery, operating at the moment of action, which is exactly where configuration-time controls run out.

Note what kind of thing the toolkit is, though, because the distinction will matter for the rest of the book. Purview, the Copilot Control System, and Entra are tenant-level surfaces; they apply to your environment because your administrators run your environment. The toolkit is a library. Engineering teams adopt it, per agent, by instrumenting it into agent code. It governs every agent whose developers volunteered. As enforcement models go, a volunteer army is better than no army, but nobody should confuse it with conscription.

Stated fairly, then: identity that makes agents visible, a schema that names an accountable human, activity capture that would satisfy a forensics team, admin controls organized into a coherent system, and an open-source enforcement engine for teams that opt in. This is the strongest first-party governance stack any platform vendor has assembled for agents. If the story ended at capability, it would end well.

*Capability note, dated: every product claim in this section was verified against Microsoft Learn or Microsoft's official blogs between July 4 and August 13, 2026. Agent-platform capabilities are currently changing quarter to quarter. The questions in the rest of this chapter are durable; re-verify the capabilities against current documentation before relying on any of them.*

## The category error

Here is where most organizations go wrong, and they go wrong in a specific, nameable way. They take the inventory above and read it as an answer to the examiner's questions. The reasoning feels sound from the inside: we bought the governance features, we configured the governance features, therefore we are governed. The reasoning fails because it mistakes one category of artifact for another. Configuration is not authorization. They are not weaker and stronger versions of the same thing. They are different kinds of thing, and no quantity of the first accumulates into the second.

Look at what a configuration actually is. A configuration describes the present state of a system: these connectors are blocked, this DLP policy applies, this label triggers that restriction. It is written by whoever holds the admin role, it changes when they change it, and it changes silently, replacing the old state without ceremony. A configuration answers the question: what can happen here?

An authorization is a different artifact answering a different question. It records a decision: a named human, on a stated date, reviewed a defined scope and accepted the risk of it on the organization's behalf. It does not describe what the system can do.

It attests that someone with the standing to decide concluded that the system should. A configuration constrains behavior. An authorization binds a person. That binding is the entire content of the artifact, and it is the content no configuration contains, because settings do not accept consequences. People do.

Every failure of governance in the first two chapters was this error wearing a different outfit. The builder at the insurer read the license as the approval: a procurement configuration, mistaken for a decision about her agent. Everyone who browsed the tenant read the populated sponsor field as accepted accountability: a directory attribute, written by a default, mistaken for an act a human performed. The organizations that greeted advisory CW1226324 with archaeology discovered that their deployment settings were their only governance record: a description of the tool, mistaken for a decision about the risk.

The error has a corporate variant that deserves its own paragraph, because it is currently being sold as the fix. Many organizations have added an AI liability addendum to their vendor contracts and consider the accountability question closed. Read what an addendum is. It configures the commercial relationship between two companies: who indemnifies whom, which warranties apply, where liability caps sit. Useful, and worth negotiating well. But it allocates the bill after something goes wrong, between corporate entities, and it names no human being inside your organization who accepted this agent's scope before it ran. When the examiner asks who authorized the agent, the addendum answers a question about who pays. The question was about who decided.

An organization can hold a flawless addendum and a perfect Purview trail and still have nobody who signed anything.

One analogy carries this distinction, and it comes from a domain that solved the problem a century ago. A modern commercial building is saturated with monitoring: cameras in the lobby, badge readers on every door, occupancy sensors, fire suppression with its own alarm log. Every one of those systems produces records, and every record is real. None of them is the permit. The permit is a separate artifact entirely: a named applicant, an approved set of plans, a defined scope of work, an inspector's signature, and a date that precedes construction. No building official has ever accepted the badge logs in place of it, and no building owner has ever thought to offer them, because a hundred years of building codes taught everyone the difference between evidence that things happened and evidence that they were approved. Agent governance is the same distinction, about thirty years behind. Most enterprises are still at the stage of pointing proudly at the sprinklers.

None of this argues that the surrounding work is wasted. Security review, privacy assessment, model validation, legal analysis, change control, and the platform controls Microsoft ships are all necessary, and an organization that skipped them would be in worse trouble than one that skipped the record. The claim is narrower and harder to dismiss. None of those activities establishes that a named person with the authority to do so decided this deployment should operate, for this purpose, within this scope, with these prohibitions. Each answers a different question well. The authorization record is where that decision becomes visible, attaches to the controls around it, and stays available to whoever has to revisit it when the deployment changes.

For most readers of this book, the obligation is not merely to oversee AI systems, assign accountability, and accept risk. It is to be able to show that those things happened. The record is the shortest path from that obligation to something an examiner can read. Who signs it, at what threshold, and what it has to contain are questions each organization answers for itself, against its own regulator, its own risk tiers, and its own delegation of authority.

## Seven questions, seven maps

Chapter 1 left seven examination questions standing. With the inventory and the category distinction in hand, each one can now be mapped precisely: what the Microsoft stack hands you, and what remains yours to build. The pattern that emerges is not seven separate gaps. It is one gap, seven times.

**How many AI agents are operating in your environment right now, and how does that number compare to the number your organization approved?** Microsoft answers the first half. The Entra directory can enumerate agent identities, and Agent 365 consolidates registry views on top of that count. The second half has no vendor answer, because the number your organization approved lives in whatever approval process your organization ran, and if no register of approved agents exists, the comparison cannot be performed by anyone. The directory gives you one column of a two-column table. Examiners are interested almost exclusively in the difference between the columns.

**For this agent: who authorized it, and what exactly was it authorized to do?** Microsoft gives you the sponsor field: a named human, machine-populated at creation, machine-maintained thereafter. What it cannot give you is the signed scope, the document stating what this agent is permitted to do and where its permission ends, reviewed and accepted by that human before go-live. The field names a person. The question asks for that person's decision, and the platform never witnessed one.

**When it acts outside that scope, which named human answers? Not a team. A name.** The owner, sponsor, and manager relationships in Entra are genuine progress here; the schema can hold the name. But holding a name and binding one are different operations. The organizational artifact is the human who accepted this agent's risks in writing, who knew they were accepting them, and who could not plausibly claim otherwise later. A schema slot filled by a default cannot survive the follow-up question, which is always: show me where they agreed.

**This outcome came from multiple agents acting in sequence. Whose authorization covers the chain?** The platform can show you the sequence, handoffs timestamped where the service supports it, each agent identified along the way. What no platform records is an approval whose scope is the chain itself: the aggregate of what three agents in sequence can do, which is reliably more than any of the three was individually approved to do. For now, note only that the topology is visible and the authorization covering it does not exist as a category of platform artifact.

**Your systems of record show the change the agent made. Can they show who sanctioned it?** Purview and the application logs answer the first sentence completely; in Dynamics 365 Business Central, a sales order agent's actions appear in document history under its own user identity, like an employee's (Microsoft Learn, verified July 4, 2026). The second sentence requires attribution above the telemetry: a record connecting this class of change to a standing, current, human-granted permission. The log shows the entry was posted. Only your governance record can show the posting was sanctioned, and only if the record exists.

**Your monitoring flagged this before the incident. What were you required to do when the flag fired, and did you do it?** Microsoft supplies the flag: Purview alerts, Defender detections, the toolkit's policy denials for instrumented agents. The obligation the flag triggers is written nowhere in the platform, because it cannot be. What your organization is required to do when a specific alert fires is a commitment your organization makes, and if it was never made, the alert simply documents that you were told. An unanswered flag is evidence with a timestamp.

**Is any of this current? When was this authorization last revisited, and what change would have forced a revisit?** Here the Microsoft column is empty, and the emptiness is honest. Nothing in the stack revisits your risk acceptance, because the stack never held your risk acceptance. Entra access reviews come closest, and they recertify the wrong object: they revisit who holds access, not whether the acceptance behind the agent still stands. Currency of authorization is organizational all the way down: a review cadence, defined triggers, evidence the review occurred. Real examinations tend to draw blood on exactly this question, because plenty of organizations that managed to produce launch paperwork cannot produce anything dated since.

Read the seven maps together and the pattern flattens into a single sentence. Microsoft reliably supplies the record of what is and what happened. The record of what was decided, by whom, and whether the decision still stands is absent in all seven, and absent for the same reason: it is testimony, not telemetry. A platform can only log the decisions your organization actually makes. Seven questions, and in most tenants, seven decisions that were never made anywhere a log could see.

## Yours by design

One suspicion remains to be retired, because it comforts a lot of roadmap-watchers: that this gap is a missing feature, and some future SKU will close it. Microsoft's own documentation retires it.

The published shared responsibility model for AI is explicit about where the lines sit. Responsibilities reside with whoever performs the task; Microsoft secures the platform layers, and the customer owns the usage layer in every deployment model, from fully managed SaaS like Microsoft 365 Copilot to custom builds on Azure (Microsoft Learn, learn.microsoft.com/en-us/azure/security/fundamentals/shared-responsibility-ai, verified August 13, 2026). Microsoft's service assurance documentation goes further: customers must establish AI governance and oversight mechanisms, and remain responsible for how AI is used within their organization even when the AI is a SaaS product Microsoft operates end to end (Microsoft Learn, learn.microsoft.com/en-us/compliance/assurance/assurance-artificial-intelligence, verified

August 13, 2026). None of this is buried. It sits in plain documentation, which in fairness is its own kind of hiding place.

Resist reading that framing as a vendor limiting its exposure, even though it also does that. Read it as an accurate statement about what authorization is. Accepting risk on an organization's behalf requires standing inside that organization: knowledge of its risk appetite, authority over its operations, exposure to its consequences. A vendor has none of those, structurally, no matter how good its tooling gets. Redmond can build you a better sponsor field every quarter. It cannot know whether the claims agent should exist, and it cannot accept what happens if the answer was no. The gap between configuration and authorization sits at the boundary of what a product can be, not in Microsoft's product line.

Which returns us to the record on the analyst's screen, and to what changes now that you have read this chapter, which is nothing, and that is the uncomfortable part. The tenant is still writing rows. Every hour, your environment produces more flawless, labeled, timestamped, legally holdable evidence of what your agents did, maintained at enterprise grade, on infrastructure you pay for. The evidence of what they were allowed to do is exactly as complete as it was the day each agent went live. For most agents, in most tenants, that means a well-lit archive of activity accumulating daily beside an authorization record that holds steady at zero pages. The ratio between those two bodies of evidence gets worse every hour the tenant is on, and every governance feature in the next Microsoft release cycle improves the wrong side of it.

Microsoft sold you the audit trail. Nobody can sell you the authorization.

The audit trail arrives with the license. The authorization has to be written by a person with something to lose, and the first thing to check in your own tenant is not whether the tooling is configured. It is whether, anywhere in the organization, a page exists that a named human would recognize, under oath, as their decision.

---

# PART 2: THE MICROSOFT AGENT STACK

Six chapters, six layers of the Microsoft agent estate, one repeating discovery. Copilot in Microsoft 365, agents built in Copilot Studio, Power Platform automation, custom builds on Azure AI and Microsoft Foundry, the Agent 365 control plane, and multi-agent chains each raise the authorization question in a different costume. The platform detail in this part moves fastest, and the note at the front of this book explains how that is handled. The question each chapter ends on will still be true when the screenshots are not.

# Chapter 4

# Microsoft 365 Copilot

The email that mattered was never opened.

In June 2025, researchers at Aim Security published a demonstration that unsettled even people who make a living being unsettled. They showed that an attacker could send a single, ordinary-looking email to an employee at any organization running Microsoft 365 Copilot, and then wait. The employee never had to open it, click anything in it, or know it existed. The email simply sat in the inbox, indistinguishable from the meeting-notes and vendor-newsletter sediment that accumulates in every mailbox, carrying instructions written not for the human recipient but for the software that would eventually read over the human's shoulder.

Then, days or weeks later, the employee would ask Copilot a routine question. Summarize where we landed on the pricing discussion. What are the key points from last month's planning threads. Copilot would do what it was built to do: reach across the mailbox, the SharePoint sites, the Teams messages, and the

OneDrive folders the employee could access, assemble the relevant material, and answer. Among the material it assembled was the attacker's email, and inside that email were the instructions. Follow them, and Copilot would locate sensitive content within its reach and transmit it outward, smuggled through channels the researchers had found ways to keep open. No click. No malware. No compromised credential. The researchers called it EchoLeak. Microsoft assigned it CVE-2025-32711, rated it critical at 9.3, described it in its advisory as "AI command injection in M365 Copilot," fixed it on the server side with no customer action required, and reported no evidence it was ever exploited in the wild (Aim Security disclosure and Microsoft Security Response Center advisory, June 2025; SecurityWeek, June 12, 2025).

As security incidents go, this one ended about as well as they end. A research team found the flaw before criminals did. The vendor patched it centrally. Nobody's data is known to have left any building. The security community wrote its analyses, coined a term for the attack class, and moved on to the next disclosure. If this were a security chapter, it would be over.

It is not a security chapter, and the reason it is not is the most important thing about EchoLeak for the people this book is written for. Look at what the fix fixed. Microsoft closed the exit: the channels through which retrieved data could leave. It did not touch, because nothing was broken about, the reach: the fact that Copilot's working scope was everything the employee could access, which is why the attack was worth mounting in the first place. The exploit needed no privilege escalation. It borrowed the scope the organization had already granted, and only that: Copilot never held rights beyond the requesting user's own identity, and the attack never needed more. That scope survived the patch fully intact, because the scope was not a vulnerability. The scope was the product.

Which raises the question the incident response never asked, because incident response is not built to ask it. Who approved that scope? Your organization has granted an AI system standing permission to retrieve and synthesize everything every licensed employee can touch. Someone, presumably, decided that. Find the decision.

## Looks like search, acts like an agent

Start with what Microsoft 365 Copilot actually does, because its deployment experience conceals it. Copilot is a retrieval system layered over the Microsoft Graph, the connective tissue that links a tenant's mail, files, chats, calendars, and meeting transcripts. When a user asks a question, Copilot searches that graph for relevant content, feeds what it finds to a language model as grounding, and generates an answer with citations back to the sources. The permission rule is simple and, to Microsoft's credit, cleanly enforced: Copilot can only summarize or reference content the requesting user is authorized to access, and for encrypted content the user must hold both view and extract rights before Copilot will touch it (Microsoft Learn, learn.microsoft.com/en-us/copilot/microsoft-365/microsoft-365-copilot-architecture-data-protection-auditing, verified August 13, 2026).

Deploying it feels like turning on a feature. Procurement negotiates licenses. IT assigns them. A rollout communication goes out with tips for writing good prompts. At no point does the process resemble what it functionally is, which is the commissioning of an autonomous retrieval actor that answers each prompt with the full read access of whoever asked, multiplied across your entire licensed workforce, operating at machine speed, on demand, thousands of times a day.

The reassurance offered at every step of that rollout is the sentence you have read in every Copilot deck: it respects existing permissions. The sentence is true. It is also the single most consequential sentence in the deployment, and almost nobody reads it as consequential, because it is phrased as a limit when it is actually a scope grant. Respects existing permissions means the scope is your permission model, all of it, as it stands, whatever state it is in. The sentence does not say your permission model is ready to be executed. It says it is about to be.

Here is the difference that matters. Before Copilot, your permission model was a paper asset. Access control lists existed, and they were consulted one door at a time, when a human happened to walk up to a specific door. An auditor sampled them annually. A security review checked the sensitive sites. The model's errors, and after fifteen years of SharePoint every model has accumulated errors, were mostly dormant, because exercising a permission required a human to know the content existed, want it, and go find it. Copilot converts the model from occasionally checked to continuously executed. Every prompt interrogates the entire reachable estate, exhaustively, without fatigue, without the faintest idea which of those permissions were deliberate and which were accidents nobody ever noticed. Search required you to know what to look for. An agent goes looking on your behalf. That is the whole distinction between the two, and it is the distinction your permission model was never designed to survive.

## Who can, and who will

Consider a site that exists, in some form, in nearly every tenant of meaningful age. Five years ago, during an open-enrollment crunch, someone on the HR team shared a compensation-planning site with the built-in group called Everyone except external users, because the deadline was Friday and group-by-group permissions were a Monday problem. The deadline passed. The Monday problem was never scheduled. The site held salary bands, equity guidance, a spreadsheet of proposed adjustments by name. And for five years, nothing happened, because nothing about the site announced itself. It appeared in no navigation anyone used. Finding it required knowing it existed. In the credential sense, four thousand employees could read it. In the practical sense, six did.

Then the tenant turned on Copilot, and an engineer two floors and one org chart away asked a perfectly reasonable question about the salary band for a senior role, and got a perfectly grounded answer, with a citation to a spreadsheet the engineer had never seen, on a site the engineer had never visited, published by people who had long since forgotten the share existed. No control failed. Every access was authorized, in the only sense of the word the platform knows. The audit log, as Chapter 3 established, recorded the whole thing beautifully.

The cleanest way to see what happened is the way governments handle classified material, which runs on two gates rather than one.

The first gate is clearance: a standing determination of what level of material a person may hold. The second is need-to-know: a specific determination that this person requires this material for this purpose. Clearance alone opens nothing. The system assumes that plenty of people are cleared for documents they have no business reading, and it interposes a second, purpose-based decision before the folder opens.

Your enterprise permission model is the clearance gate. The need-to-know gate was never built. What stood in its place, unplanned and unexamined, was friction: the sheer difficulty of discovering content in a sprawling estate. Obscurity was performing need-to-know's job, badly but pervasively, across millions of files. It appeared on no control inventory, carried no owner, and cost nothing, which is why nobody noticed it was load-bearing. Copilot removed it. Tenant-wide. On a date you can look up in your deployment plan. Copilot didn't change who can see the file. It changed who will.

And here is the governance point hiding inside the mechanism: the removal of that layer was never authorized, because the layer itself never had been. You cannot find the signature that accepted the risk of retiring a control that no document ever admitted was a control. The deployment approval, wherever it lives, approved a productivity tool. It did not approve the end of obscurity, because nobody in the approval chain understood that obscurity was in service. This is not a failure anyone can be blamed for individually, which is what makes it an institutional failure. The decision was real, the consequences were material, and no human being ever visibly made it.

## The standing approval

Microsoft understands this problem, and it deserves credit for saying so in public documentation rather than in fine print. Its own deployment guidance opens with the premise that tenants harbor oversharing and must remediate it before Copilot scales. The blueprint it publishes is genuinely prescriptive: use Purview's data security posture management for AI to find overshared sites holding sensitive content; run the Content Management Assessment in SharePoint Advanced Management, which is included with the Copilot license, to surface sites with oversized audiences and broken permission inheritance; apply Restricted Content Discovery to hide high-risk sites from Copilot and organization-wide search while owners review them; send site access reviews to the owners who actually know who needs what; lock business-critical sites behind Restricted Access Control; and let data loss prevention policies keep labeled sensitive content out of Copilot's grounding altogether (Microsoft Learn, learn.microsoft.com/en-us/copilot/microsoft-365/microsoft-365-copilot-blueprint-oversharing and learn.microsoft.com/en-us/sharepoint/restricted-content-discovery and learn.microsoft.com/en-us/microsoft-365/copilot/configure-secure-governed-data-foundation-microsoft-365-copilot, verified July 10, 2026, re-verified August 13, 2026). As of late 2026 this tooling is real, shipping, and unusually complete for the same problem; current feature boundaries, license tiers, console procedures, and the technical anatomy of the EchoLeak bypass chain live in this book's companion annex rather than here, because they will have changed by the time you read this and the questions below will not have.

Notice, before moving on, one small honesty in the documentation. Microsoft describes Restricted Content Discovery as a temporary governance control, a way to buy time while permissions get reviewed. An earlier control in the same family, Restricted SharePoint Search, wore the same temporary label and is now being retired outright, new enablement blocked from July 31, 2026 (Microsoft Learn, learn.microsoft.com/sharepoint/restricted-sharepoint-search, verified August 13, 2026). Temporary is doing hopeful work in those sentences. In enterprise configuration, temporary is less a duration than a genre, and a fair number of the sites restricted during 2026 rollouts will still be restricted when the administrators who restricted them have left for other jobs. What those tenants will be running, by then, is a semi-permanent shadow scope: real, enforced daily, and documented nowhere as a business decision.

Every item in that inventory is a setting, and Chapter 3 already established what settings are and are not, so the point gets one sentence here: the blueprint can contain your exposure, and no step in it produces a record of a named human deciding the exposure was acceptable. What the blueprint cannot generate, only your organization can. Four questions, in print because they will outlast every screenshot.

First. Who approved the retrieval scope? Not the purchase, the scope. In most organizations the license procurement stood in for the scope decision, which means the effective approval reads: whatever the permission model happens to contain, executed at machine speed, for every licensed user. If a named person examined that proposition and accepted it, the organization has an answer. If the scope simply rode in with the invoice, it has a purchase order.

Second. Who approved the exclusions? An exclusion list is one of the most revealing documents an organization can produce, because it is a written admission of where the organization does not trust its own permissions. Somebody decided which sites went on it, which is also a decision about every site that stayed off. In practice that decision was usually made by an administrator, under rollout deadline, in a console, and recorded as a configuration change rather than as what it was: a risk acceptance about everything not listed. Sensitivity labels and data loss prevention policies do not rescue the record, either; they subtract defined classes of labeled content from the scope, and the unlabeled majority of most estates rides the default.

Third. Who monitors drift under the standing approval? Whatever was approved was approved against the tenant as it stood on a date. The tenant did not hold still. Every share link, every new site, every group membership change since that date has silently amended the scope, because the approval attached to the permission model and the permission model is a living thing. A site created tomorrow morning and shared with Everyone except external users enters Copilot's reach at creation, pre-approved by a signature that predates its existence. Site access reviews do not answer this; they recertify who belongs to a site when someone thinks to initiate one, and nothing binds their schedule to the approval whose currency is in question. An approval that automatically covers things that did not exist when it was signed is not an approval. It is a subscription.

Fourth. Who owns the oversharing posture as a standing condition? The remediation blueprint runs as a project, and it should. But projects end. The Content Management Assessment gets run, the reviews get sent, the readiness milestone gets marked complete, and the team disbands to the next initiative. The condition the project created begins decaying the following Monday, at the rate your organization creates content, which is to say constantly. Somewhere between the CISO, the SharePoint service owner, the data governance lead, and the Copilot product owner, the clean posture is assumed to be somebody's ongoing job. Chapter 2 described what that particular arrangement of assumptions produces.

The pattern across all four is the same, and it is this chapter's version of the split this book keeps finding. The permission check is continuous: enforced on every retrieval, by the platform, flawlessly. The permission decision is frozen: made once, if at all, against a snapshot that stopped being true before the rollout email finished sending. Microsoft's machinery keeps the check current. Nothing keeps the decision current, because the decision does not live in the machinery.

## The question the patch can't reach

Return, at the end, to EchoLeak, because its afterlife is instructive. The vulnerability was handled the way the security discipline handles things, which is to say competently: classified, patched, written up, absorbed into the canon of attack techniques with a name and a CVE number. Every artifact of that response exists and can be produced on demand. The advisory. The patch confirmation. The internal ticket where your security team verified there was nothing for them to do.

Now run the other inquiry, the one this book keeps running. An examiner, or a plaintiff's counsel, or your own board after some future incident that does not end as harmlessly, asks a question no CVE database can answer. Your organization granted an AI system standing authority to retrieve and synthesize everything every employee can reach, including the accumulated permission accidents of fifteen years, and the researchers have demonstrated that this reach is exactly what an attacker rents when the next bypass is found. Show us the decision to grant it. Not the license agreement. Not the rollout plan. Not the readiness checklist. The record of a named human being who understood that scope, weighed it, and accepted it on the organization's behalf, and the record of when anyone last looked again.

Most organizations will reach for the deployment approval and discover, reading it closely for the first time, that it approved a product and inherited a scope. The scope came from a permission model built across two decades for a world where reading a file required a person to go get it, a world that ended, tenant by tenant, on whatever date Copilot went live. The end of that world produced no paperwork. It could not have. You cannot sign the retirement of a control you never admitted you were relying on.

Tomorrow morning, somewhere in your tenant, a project lead with a Friday deadline will create a new site and share it with everyone, just for now. It will enter the approved scope the moment they click save. Whoever signed that approval has never heard of the site, the project, or the lead. In every meaningful sense they approved it anyway. That is the arrangement currently in force, and it renews itself daily, and the only signature on it is old.

## THE RECORD THIS CHAPTER REQUIRES

| | |
|---|---|
| **What the platform proves** | Every retrieval was permitted. Copilot honored the permission model on each request, and the Purview audit record shows which user prompted, what was returned, and when. |
| **What it does not prove** | That anyone examined the scope those permissions describe. A permission check confirms access was allowed. It does not confirm a person decided it should be. |
| **What the organization must decide** | The retrieval scope as a scope, separately from the purchase. What is in reach, what is excluded, and on whose authority. |
| **The record that must exist** | A named person's acceptance of the retrieval scope as it stood on a stated date, with the exclusion list attached as part of the decision rather than filed as a configuration change. |
| **What reopens it** | Any change that widens reach without passing through the approval: a site shared broadly, a group membership change, the retirement of a containment control, or a platform change to what grounding can see. |

# Chapter 5

# Copilot Studio Agents

Nobody in the audience thought he was bluffing, because he brought the scan results.

In August 2024, at the Black Hat security conference in Las Vegas, a researcher named Michael Bargury, chief technology officer of the security firm Zenity, presented a talk titled "15 Ways to Break Your Copilot." Its centerpiece was not an exotic exploit. It was a census. His team had scanned the public internet for agents built with Microsoft Copilot Studio, the low-code tool that lets employees with no programming background assemble AI agents on top of company data, and found tens of thousands of them sitting on the open web, answerable to anyone who found them, no login required. The cause was not a breach. It was a default: at the time, Copilot Studio's settings published agents to the web without requiring authentication, and thousands of organizations had shipped agents without changing that setting, or knowing it existed (The Register, August 8, 2024).

The team went further. In its published research summary, Zenity reported finding more than a thousand such agents belonging to Fortune 500 companies, and demonstrated that a determined visitor could extract sensitive material from them, including legal documents, by doing nothing more sophisticated than asking persistently and creatively (Zenity Labs research summary, Black Hat USA 2024). Bargury's group released a scanning tool, CopilotHunter, so organizations could find their own exposed agents before someone else did, and told The Register that in the average large enterprise, its data showed nearly three thousand Copilot Studio agents in operation, a majority of them discoverable online (Zenity's own figures, reported by The Register, August 8, 2024, and not independently replicated; the argument of this chapter survives if the census runs smaller). Microsoft, which Bargury publicly credited as responsive throughout the disclosure, changed the default so that new deployments no longer published to the open internet unauthenticated. Agents deployed before the change kept whatever settings they had. Organizations were advised to go check (The Register, August 8, 2024).

The security community processed this the way it processes everything: attack surface, misconfiguration, remediation, conference applause. And on those terms the story resolves. The default got fixed. The tool exists. The scan can be run.

But sit with the census number rather than the exposure, because the number is the part that survives every patch. Thousands of agents per large enterprise. Before Bargury could find agents that were accidentally public, someone had to build them, and the building is the part nobody presented a talk about, because the building was working exactly as designed. Every one of those agents was created by an employee, on licensed software, connected to company data through dialogs the employee clicked through, and placed into service. The exposure was a misconfiguration. The existence was the product. And if you ask, for any one of those thousands of agents, the question this book keeps asking, which named person decided this agent should exist and do what it does, the honest answer at most organizations is that the question assumes a decision process the agent never passed through. Not because it was smuggled around the process. Because no process was ever put in its path.

## The maker layer

Copilot Studio's premise, stated plainly, is that building an AI agent should be about as hard as building a PowerPoint deck. An employee opens a design surface, types instructions in plain English, points the agent at knowledge sources such as SharePoint sites, uploaded files, or Dataverse tables, wires it to systems through prebuilt connectors, and publishes it to Teams, to a website, or into Microsoft 365 Copilot. Microsoft calls these employees makers. The term is precise. They are not developers, not IT, not a project team. They are the claims analyst, the HR generalist, the finance manager who got tired of answering the same question forty times a week.

This is genuinely valuable, and pretending otherwise would be dishonest about why organizations buy it. The people closest to a broken process are the best qualified to describe what a fix should do, and for decades the bottleneck was that describing a fix and building one were different professions. Copilot Studio collapses them. The cost of that collapse is the subject of this chapter, and the cost is not technical. Every maker is now, functionally, an internal software vendor, shipping systems into your operating environment, and your organization has met exactly none of them the way it meets vendors.

Consider how your company treats money, because money is the risk it has governed longest and best. A seventy-five-dollar team lunch requires a receipt, a cost code, and a manager's click in the expense system. Five thousand dollars of software requires a director. A quarter million brings procurement, security review, legal, and a signature chain that takes six weeks. Nobody resents this, much, because the thresholds encode an old and sound principle: as the amount of risk climbs, the seniority of the person accepting it climbs with it. The entire apparatus rests on one input, an amount, presented up front, that routes the request to the right level of authority.

Agent creation shipped with no amount. An agent that answers vacation-policy questions from the employee handbook and an agent that reads the customer database and drafts outbound email present identically at the moment of creation: as nothing, a free action inside an already-licensed tool. There is no field on the Create screen where risk is denominated, so there is no threshold to trip, so the request routes nowhere. The agent with standing access to your CRM clears every approval gate your company has, at every level, simultaneously, by never presenting anything a gate could evaluate. Your expense system would stop the lunch. The maker built it in an afternoon. Your approval process assumed a project.

That last assumption deserves to be said carefully, because it is the actual mechanism of the gap. Enterprise approval processes are not missing; they are aimed. They aim at projects: things with budgets, kickoffs, staffing requests, vendor contracts, go-live dates. Every one of those artifacts is a tripwire that summons oversight. Copilot Studio's entire value proposition is the removal of those artifacts. No budget line, no kickoff, no staffing, no contract, no date. The governance apparatus is intact, functioning, and pointed at a doorway the work no longer walks through.

## The sponsor who never consented

Here is where the Microsoft stack does something remarkable, and where reading it carefully matters more than anywhere else in this chapter.

When an employee creates an agent in Copilot Studio today, the platform automatically creates an identity for that agent in the organization's Microsoft Entra directory, the same directory that holds every employee's account. Microsoft's documentation states it directly: each time an agent is created, it receives an agent identity in the tenant, and "the user who created the agent is recorded as its sponsor" (Microsoft Learn, learn.microsoft.com/en-us/entra/agent-id/what-are-agent-identities, verified August 13, 2026). The sponsor, as Chapter 2 established from the same documentation, is the directory's word for the accountable human, the one answerable for the agent's purpose and lifecycle. Chapter 2 watched what happens when other people read that field and mistake a populated attribute for a completed decision. This chapter is about the person whose name is in the field.

Ask what she did to acquire the role. She clicked Create. That is the complete ceremony. The screen did not describe sponsorship, define its obligations, or ask whether she accepted them. No enterprise message told her afterward that a directory now lists her as the accountable human for a piece of operating software. The role attached to her the way lint attaches to a jacket, as a side effect of walking through the room.

Now hold that next to how your organization confers every other accountable role it takes seriously. Employment begins with an offer letter, signed. Signing authority is delegated in a written instrument with a dollar limit. Officers of the company accept appointment formally. The on-call engineer acknowledges the rotation in the paging tool. Even the mundane end of accountability runs on assent: annual conflict-of-interest attestations, policy acknowledgments, the compliance training with the button that says I understand my obligations. Your organization spends real money every year on software whose only job is collecting these acceptances, because mature control systems have learned that accountability which was never accepted does not hold when pulled. This quarter, in your building, a coordinator will spend two weeks chasing directors to sign their attestations. Sponsorship of an AI agent is assigned in less time than the confirmation toast takes to fade.

The trap to avoid here is thinking the maker consented because she clicked through consent screens. She did click consent dialogs, real ones, when the agent connected to data sources, and Chapter 2's builder read hers carefully. But look at what those dialogs ask. They ask whether the agent may access resources, under permissions the maker already holds. They are consent to capability. Nothing in the flow is consent to answerability, the acceptance of being the named human who explains this agent to an examiner in three years. The process collects a signature, and it is the wrong signature: it authorizes the agent to act and leaves unsigned the question of who answers for the acting. Chapter 3 spent its whole length on why a configuration record cannot stand in for that acceptance, and the point transfers here whole.

Be fair to the machinery before leaving it, because a sharp reader will raise the objection. The directory does not stop at recording a sponsor. Microsoft Entra ID Governance can build real process on the attribute: sponsors can be assigned deliberately after creation, agents can receive access through access packages with expiry dates, and when an assignment nears expiration, the sponsor is notified and must choose between requesting an extension, which can trigger a fresh approval cycle, and letting the access lapse (Microsoft Learn, learn.microsoft.com/en-us/entra/id-governance/agent-id-governance-overview, verified August 13, 2026). An organization that wants a sponsorship ceremony can construct one from these parts. That is the right way to read the platform, and it concedes nothing, because constructing the ceremony is a decision your organization has to make, staff, and document, and the platform will never make it for you. Out of the box, the field populates without it. An examiner will treat the populated sponsor attribute as an input to the accountability question, not as evidence that accountability was ever consciously accepted, and the distance between those two readings is your organization's to close.

One more fact from the documentation, easy to skim past and heavy once weighed. Automatic identity creation has a start date and, until recently, had an off switch. Microsoft's migration guidance marks March 18, 2026 as the point at which Copilot Studio began automatically creating agent identities for new agents, in environments where the capability is enabled; the companion admin documentation described a temporary environment-level opt-out, and has since closed it: starting July 2026, agent identities are mandatory for all new agents, and the opt-out is gone (Microsoft Learn, learn.microsoft.com/en-us/entra/agent-id/migrate-copilot-studio-agents-to-agent-id and learn.microsoft.com/en-us/microsoft-copilot-studio/admin-use-entra-agent-identities, verified August 13, 2026). Agents created before that date, or in environments that opted out, run on legacy app registrations that the directory treats as standard applications, not as AI agents, and there is today no in-place migration, only a rebuild, though the documentation now promises an automatic migration to come and tells organizations not to recreate production-critical agents in the meantime (same migration guidance, re-verified August 13, 2026). The documentation adds, in its even way, that "some preexisting agents might not have sponsors yet" (Microsoft Learn, learn.microsoft.com/en-us/microsoft-copilot-studio/requirements-certificates-configuration-values, verified August 13, 2026). Read as an examiner would: everything your makers built during the two years of heaviest experimentation, the entire 2024 and 2025 vintage that Bargury's scanner was finding, is invisible to the directory as an agent population and may carry no accountable name at all, not even an unconsenting one. The platform's automatic accountability is real, and it is arriving in stages, and your fleet predates it.

## Autonomy on the maker's badge

Everything so far describes agents that answer when spoken to. Copilot Studio's trajectory, like the industry's, points somewhere else: agents that act because something happened, with no human in the conversation at all.

The platform calls these event triggers. A maker can configure an agent to wake when an email arrives, a file appears, a database row changes, or simply on a schedule, and then carry out its instructions, calling connectors and taking actions, unattended (Microsoft Learn, learn.microsoft.com/en-us/microsoft-copilot-studio/authoring-triggers-about, verified August 13, 2026). This is where an agent stops resembling a chatbot and starts resembling a process, and the documentation contains a sentence that every CISO reading this should go verify personally: for an agent to run autonomously, its triggers and authenticated actions currently use the maker's credentials. The same page warns makers, before publishing, that users of such an agent might reach information or perform actions through the author's credentials, and notes that administrators can block event triggers outright (Microsoft Learn, same page, verified August 13, 2026).

Slow that down. In default configurations today, the unattended process handling live business events runs on the personal authority of whichever employee assembled it, and the risk disclosure for that arrangement is delivered as a dialog to the one person in the chain with the least organizational standing to accept it. Microsoft has shipped the corrective control: administrators can now restrict maker-provided credentials per environment or environment group, forcing tools to run under each end user's own identity instead, though the setting is not enabled by default (Microsoft Learn, learn.microsoft.com/en-us/microsoft-copilot-studio/configure-no-maker-authentication, verified August 13, 2026). Enable it, and the same documentation is candid about the consequence: agents that run on schedules or wake to events fail, because every tool call now requires a live sign-in and "all agent triggers must involve an active user" (Microsoft Learn, same page, verified August 13, 2026). The tenant is offered a clean choice between autonomous agents on borrowed personal credentials and no autonomous agents, and choosing between those is a risk acceptance, not a settings decision. It is being made today, in most tenants, by whoever left the default alone. The maker, meanwhile, is being asked to consent, on the spot, to something that is not hers to consent to: the standing exposure of her credentials' full reach to whatever the agent does unattended. She clicks through, because the dialog is phrased as a technical note and the deadline is Thursday. Inside that click, the organization acquired an unattended system acting as a person, and the acquisition was approved by nobody, unless that dialog counts as your approval process. In a default-configuration tenant, it is currently the only one in the path.

## What the console can say

Microsoft has not been idle about any of this, and the fair accounting matters, because the pattern it reveals is the book's pattern. Administrators today have real machinery. Sharing controls in the Power Platform admin center let admins restrict which makers can share agents, with whom, and at what scale, applied per environment or across environment groups (Microsoft Learn, learn.microsoft.com/en-us/microsoft-copilot-studio/admin-sharing-controls-limits, verified August 13, 2026). Data loss prevention policies decide which connectors agents may use in which environments. Publishing of generative AI agents can be disabled tenant-wide (Microsoft Learn, learn.microsoft.com/en-us/microsoft-copilot-studio/security-and-governance, verified August 13, 2026). When a maker publishes an agent with an agent identity, the connectors it can call are attached to that identity as API permissions, visible to admins in the Entra admin center. And the Microsoft 365 admin center now shows an Agent Registry: a screen listing shared agents with name, creator, creation date, and where each one runs (Microsoft Learn, learn.microsoft.com/en-us/microsoft-365/admin/manage/manage-copilot-agents-integrated-apps, verified August 13, 2026). As of late 2026 this is a genuinely capable console, and it is improving quarterly; fast-decaying detail for this surface lives in the companion annex, per the note at the front of this book, and the questions below will outlast all of it.

You can hear the shape of the sentence coming, because Chapters 3 and 4 built it. Every item in that inventory is a control on what makers can do. None of it is a record of what the organization decided a specific agent should do. Some mature tenants already repurpose these surfaces as improvised approval gates, requiring, say, a security sign-off before an agent may be shared beyond its builder's team, and the instinct is sound as far as it goes. But a gate on distribution is not a decision about existence, purpose, or knowledge scope, and what the gate leaves behind in the record is a configuration change with a ticket number, not an accepted risk with a name. The registry is an attendance sheet, not an approval log. The sharing limit is a wall, not a decision. An examiner who asks who authorized this agent can be shown the environment policy under which it was buildable, which answers a different question, the same different question it answered in the last two chapters.

## Five questions for the agent your analyst built

So put the questions in print, where the console updates cannot reach them.

First. Who approved this agent's existence? Not the Copilot Studio license, not the environment it was built in. This agent. If the answer is that creation inside a licensed environment is implicit approval, then your organization's position is that it pre-approved every agent any employee will ever build, sight unseen, and someone senior should confirm in writing that this is the position.

Second. Who approved what it knows and says? An agent's topic scope and knowledge sources are decisions about what the organization will assert to whoever asks. The maker pointed it at a SharePoint site; who confirmed the site contains only what the agent's audience should receive, and who is watching what gets added to that site next month? The agent's answers are only as authorized as its sources, and its sources are a living folder.

Third. Who holds the connector inventory? Every connector is standing reach into a business system. The permissions exist in the platform and, for current agents, on the agent's identity, so the list is producible. Producible is not the question. Reviewed is the question: which named human looked at this agent's specific combination of reach, the customer table plus the email connector plus the file store, and accepted what the combination can do? Combinations are where agents get interesting, and where nobody is looking.

Fourth. What may it do with no human in the loop? For any agent with triggers: which of its actions execute unattended, on whose credentials, and who other than the maker decided that this process may run as that person indefinitely? If the answer to the credential question surprises whoever owns identity in your organization, that is worth knowing on a calm Tuesday rather than during an incident.

Fifth. Where is the line between a personal tool and departmental infrastructure, and who is watching for the crossing? Every consequential maker-built agent begins as somebody's convenience. Then a teammate asks for the link, then it is pinned in the Teams channel, then a manager cites its answers in a decision, and a few quarters later a business process quietly depends on software that is still, in every record that exists, one person's afternoon experiment. Your organization has crossing rules for money: the moment a purchase exceeds a threshold, it changes category and gains oversight. Agents have no denominated amount, so this question is asking you to invent the threshold, name it, and assign someone to notice when an agent crosses it. Nobody else will, because the crossing has no sound.

Return once more to Las Vegas, because the census deserves a final reading. Bargury had to scan the internet to find the agents nobody meant to expose. Nobody has to scan anything to find the agents nobody meant to authorize. They are in the registry now, at least the recent ones, each row carrying a name, a creation date, and a sponsor field filled in by machinery, listing an employee who has never been told she is listed. The exposed agents were a defect, and Microsoft fixed it. The unauthorized agents are not a defect, and Microsoft cannot fix it, because from the platform's side of the line there is nothing broken: every one of them was built by a permitted person in a permitted place with permitted connections. What is missing is missing on your side. Thousands of times over, in the average large tenant, somebody's afternoon is now part of your operating environment, and the question of who agreed to that has an answer, and the answer is a default.

## THE RECORD THIS CHAPTER REQUIRES

| | |
|---|---|
| **What the platform proves** | Which maker built the agent, in which environment, on which connectors and knowledge sources, and that the build was recorded. |
| **What it does not prove** | That anyone besides the maker agreed the agent should exist, or that the person carried as its sponsor knew they had been named. |
| **What the organization must decide** | Whether this agent is authorized. Not the license, not the environment. What it may assert, which connectors it holds, and which of its actions run with no human in the loop. |
| **The record that must exist** | A sponsor's acceptance of the topic scope, knowledge sources, connector inventory, and unattended actions, signed by someone other than the maker. |
| **What reopens it** | A new connector, a new knowledge source, a new trigger, a change of maker, or the maker's departure. |

# Chapter 6

# Power Platform Automation

The data was not stolen. It was published.

In August 2021, researchers at the security firm UpGuard disclosed that more than a thousand lists of business data, spread across several hundred web portals built on Microsoft Power Apps, were sitting on the open internet, readable by anyone who requested them. No exploit was involved. Power Apps portals could expose data through a standard web feed, and unless an administrator configured table permissions, that feed answered anonymous requests. Across the portals UpGuard examined, roughly 38 million records were reachable this way, and the contents were not test data. They included COVID-19 contact tracing records, vaccination appointment sign-ups, Social Security numbers submitted by job applicants, and employee identification numbers. UpGuard notified 47 affected organizations, among them the state governments of Indiana and Maryland, the city of New York, American Airlines, Ford, J.B. Hunt, and Microsoft itself, whose Global Payroll Services portal exposed 332,000 records about its own workforce (UpGuard Research disclosure, "By Design," August 23, 2021; The Register, August 23, 2021).

The timeline inside that disclosure is the part worth slowing down for. UpGuard found the first exposed portal in May 2021 and filed a report with the Microsoft Security Response Center on June 24. Five days later Microsoft closed the case, telling the researchers the behavior was "considered to be by design" (UpGuard disclosure, reported by TechRepublic, August 23, 2021). The company was not wrong. The product documentation described exactly what happened when the permissions were left unset. Every one of those portals was operating precisely as configured. After further reports, Microsoft notified affected customers, changed the platform so that table permissions are enabled by default on new portals, and shipped a tool for customers to check existing ones. A Microsoft spokesperson noted that only a small subset of customers had configured portals this way (TechRepublic, August 25, 2021). No public evidence at the time of disclosure indicated the data had been misused (The Register, August 23, 2021).

Notice what kind of failure this was, because it was not a breach and it was not a bug. Forty-seven organizations were operating public data feeds that none of them had decided to operate. Each one was running a platform whose default disagreed with an assumption nobody had ever been assigned to check. The fix Microsoft shipped was a changed default, and it worked, and the whole episode closed years before most of those organizations had deployed anything they would call AI.

That is why this chapter opens in 2021. This book is about AI agents, and Power Platform is the layer of the Microsoft stack where the book's question turns out to predate its subject. The governance debt was in the substrate before the models arrived. Your organization did not acquire an ungoverned population of autonomous actors when it turned on Copilot. It acquired the platform for building them years earlier, ran thousands, and called them productivity.

## The automation nobody counts

Strip a Power Automate flow down to what it does and describe it without the product name. A piece of standing logic watches for a condition: a schedule, an email arriving in a mailbox, a row changing in a database, a form being submitted. When the condition fires, it acts, across systems, through authenticated connections, without a human present. It sends the email, updates the record, posts the message, moves the file, files the approval request. It does this at two in the afternoon and two in the morning, on weekends, during the owner's parental leave, at whatever pace its triggers dictate.

Described that way, the flow is an agent in every sense this book has used the word except one: there is no model inside it. Its logic is fixed rather than generated. Determinism is a fact about how the flow decides, not about what its decisions touch. A flow with no model can still screen a payment against a sanctions list, escalate an exception that a control framework treats as a signing event, or send a regulated customer a notice that carries legal weight. To an examiner, the presence or absence of a model in the loop is not the question. The question is whether anyone authorized the action the loop takes. And that single difference, model or no model, has done a remarkable amount of definitional work in enterprise governance, because when organizations began building AI agent inventories, agent review boards, and agent risk frameworks in 2025 and 2026, the flow fleet sat outside all of them, doing the same category of thing the definitions were written to govern: taking actions in business systems under standing authority, on behalf of people who are not watching.

The population is not small and it is not new. Power Automate has been shipping for the better part of a decade under one name or another, seeded into Microsoft 365 licenses most enterprises already own, which means the typical tenant's flow fleet has been accumulating that entire time, built by the same makers Chapter 5 described, one useful automation at a time. Nobody launched this fleet. It sedimented. And each flow in it runs on connections, which is the detail the rest of this chapter turns on. A connection is an authenticated link between the platform and a system such as Outlook, SharePoint, SQL Server, or Dataverse, and it is created by a person consenting with their own credentials. The flow acts through the connection. Which means the flow acts, durably and repeatedly, as someone. Every flow in your tenant is a standing instruction executing under a human being's identity, and the human being's ongoing involvement consists of having once clicked through a dialog.

Chapter 3 established what the platform's records can and cannot prove, and there is no need to restage that argument for this layer. The point here is prior to it. Before asking whether anyone authorized the flow, notice that your organization has probably never asked how many flows there are, because flows were filed under a heading, workplace productivity, that no governance program has ever considered its business. The debt compounded because it was booked to an account nobody audits.

## The flow that outlived its owner

Watch one flow across three years, because the lifecycle is where this layer's version of the accountability gap stops being abstract. What follows is a constructed lifecycle, built to match the way these flows are built and abandoned in practice rather than drawn from any specific real firm, and every step in it uses a mechanism your tenant already runs.

In 2023, an analyst in the financial operations group of a mid-sized firm builds a flow. Every night it reads the settlement-exceptions mailbox, writes each exception into a tracking list, posts a summary to the team's channel, and, when an exception crosses a dollar threshold, files an approval request to the group's manager. The connections behind it, to the mailbox, the list, and Teams, are hers, created with her credentials in the space of a few consent dialogs. The flow is good. Exceptions stop falling through the cracks. Within a quarter the team's morning routine is built around the summary post, the way morning routines quietly reorganize themselves around anything reliable.

In 2024 she transfers to another division. Her successor inherits her caseload, her distribution lists, and her seat in the Monday meeting. Nobody inherits the flow, because the flow appears on no list of things she is handing over. It does not need her, in any operational sense. Her account remains active, as accounts often do through an internal move, since mail forwarding and shared responsibilities carry the handover and nothing forces a deactivation. Her connections keep authenticating, and the platform's documentation is precise about why this is uneventful: a flow starts failing when its owner's identity stops being valid, and hers never stopped being valid (Microsoft Learn, manage orphaned flows, learn.microsoft.com/en-us/troubleshoot/power-platform/power-automate/flow-management/manage-orphan-flow-when-owner-leaves-org, verified August 13, 2026). She has not thought about the flow in months. It posts its summary every morning to a team she no longer works on, signed, in every log line, by her.

In 2026 she resigns. Offboarding disables her account on a Friday at five. On Monday the exceptions are unprocessed, the summary post is missing, and by ten there is a priority ticket. A Power Platform administrator opens the admin center, finds the flow in the environment's resource list with its Owners column empty, and lands, as thousands of administrators have before, on the Microsoft Learn article for exactly this situation. The article is genuinely helpful. It explains that an orphaned flow is one with no valid owner, that such flows can fail when their connections are tied to the departed account, and that an administrator can assign a co-owner who can fix the connections and re-enable the flow, maintaining continuity in the automated business process. The administrator does all of this. A teammate is made co-owner, the connections are re-created under the teammate's credentials, and the flow is running again by lunch. The ticket closes. Everyone involved did their job well.

Now count what happened. Over three years, this flow's relationship to human authority was examined exactly once, for two hours, under a priority ticket, by an administrator whose mandate was to make it run again. The questions that examination answered were operational: what stopped, whose credentials, how to restore. The question this book keeps asking, who decided this flow should exist and does that decision still stand, was not skipped. It was never in scope, at any point, for anyone, because no artifact existed anywhere that the question could have been asked of. The flow was never approved, so its approval could never be revisited, transferred, or retired. It simply ran, and when running became impossible, the organization's entire institutional response was aimed at making it run again. The flow has run for three years. Its owner left two years ago. And the truest thing you can say about its governance is that the organization has now intervened in its life exactly once, to save it.

Read Microsoft's orphaned-flow documentation again with an examiner's eyes and you will notice what genre it belongs to. It is a business continuity article, and fairly so; its job is to keep automations running, and it does that job well. But set its frame beside an examiner's frame and the two invert. To the documentation, a flow that stops is the problem. To an examiner, a flow that never stops, and that no one decided should run, is the problem.

The organizations furthest along do not wait for the Monday ticket. Microsoft built tooling for exactly this, and mature shops run it: a scheduled process that finds flows whose owner has left, locates that person's former manager, and sends the manager a prompt asking what to do with the abandoned automations (Microsoft Learn, use governance components, learn.microsoft.com/en-us/power-platform/guidance/coe/governance-components, verified August 13, 2026). The choices it offers are clean. Take ownership. Reassign it to someone else. Delete it. Email yourself the list. Every one of those is a decision about who holds the flow or whether it survives. None of them is the decision this book keeps asking about. The manager is not shown what the flow does, why it was built, what risk it carries, or who authorized it, because the process does not carry those facts, because nobody recorded them. The best available version of orphaned-flow governance routes the flow to a human and asks that human to dispose of it. It cannot ask whether the flow should have existed, because that question has no record to consult.

## The key that was never returned

The analyst's offboarding, it should be said, was flawless. Badge collected, laptop returned, account disabled on schedule, access reviews clean. Identity governance did everything identity governance is designed to do, and this chapter's failure happened anyway, because the thing that persisted was never an identity. It was a delegation.

Think of every flow a person builds as a key they have cut and fitted into the building's machinery, a key that turns on a schedule whether or not they are in the building. Offboarding is built to retrieve what was issued to the person: the badge, the devices, the accounts. It has no line item for the keys the person cut themselves, because no issuance record exists for those; the platform let them cut as many as they needed, and the whole point of cutting them was that doors would open without anyone standing there. When the analyst moved divisions, her keys kept turning for two years. When she left and her badge died, the organization did not remove her keys. It called a locksmith and re-cut them onto a colleague's blank, so the doors would keep opening on schedule. At no point did anyone walk the building asking why each door needed to open nightly, because the keys were the only record of the doors, and keys do not explain themselves.

Microsoft's own guidance completes this picture in a way worth quoting rather than paraphrasing, because the guidance is sound and its governance implication is unstated. For critical or long-running flows, the documentation recommends ownership by a service principal rather than a person, so that flows "continue to run smoothly even if employees leave the company" (Microsoft Learn, flow ownership models, learn.microsoft.com/en-us/power-automate/guidance/coding-guidelines/understand-access-to-flows, verified August 13, 2026). As engineering advice this is correct, and organizations that follow it will suffer fewer Monday-morning tickets. As governance, notice what it removes. The remedy for a flow that keeps outliving its humans is to take the human out of the flow's lifecycle entirely, and it works. What it also does, unless the organization deliberately puts something back, is engineer away the last natural moment at which anyone would have looked at the flow and asked whether it should still exist: the moment it broke. Nothing about a service principal stops an organization from wrapping the flow in scheduled review and periodic re-authorization. Nothing about it requires them to, either, and the platform will never raise the question on its own, because the question used to arrive as a failure, and failure is the thing that was just fixed. The flow can now run forever. Whether anyone still answers for it is a separate question, and the machinery no longer forces it.

## Five questions for the layer nobody is examining yet

The questions this layer owes an authorization record are the same shape as the previous two chapters', and they are printed here in the same spirit: as questions your organization can answer now, on its own calendar, or be asked during an incident, and the choice of occasion is still open.

First, who owns each flow, and be precise about what that word is doing. The platform's answer is an owners list: a creator plus any co-owners, each of whom holds full control, including the power to edit, disable, or delete the flow (Microsoft Learn, sharing cloud flows,
learn.microsoft.com/en-us/power-automate/create-team-flows, verified August 13, 2026). That is an access list. It records who can touch the flow, which is a different fact from who answers for it, and the previous chapters have already established how far apart those two facts can drift. A flow with four co-owners has four people who can kill it and, in most organizations, zero people who would say in a meeting that it is theirs.

Second, what triggers it. The trigger is the flow's job description, the complete statement of when it is permitted to act, and it was written once, by its maker, and has been reviewed since by nobody. Triggers deserve particular attention wherever they fire on inbound content, a mailbox, a form, a file drop, because a flow triggered by arriving content is a flow whose workload is partly composed by strangers.

Third, what data crosses what boundaries, and reserve the closest attention for the regulated crossings: personnel data reaching an outbound mail connector, health or claims records landing in a system that sits outside the rules that govern them, customer data from one jurisdiction moving through infrastructure in another. A flow's connections routinely span systems governed by different owners, and each crossing was consented to by one person in a connection dialog. Your data loss prevention policies constrain which connectors may be combined, and they matter, but a DLP policy is a fence around the whole environment. It records what all makers are forbidden to do. It says nothing about whether this particular flow's particular crossing was ever anyone's decision.

Fourth, who reviews the flow when it fails, and sit with the corollary: for most flows, failure review is the only review there is. The flow that breaks gets two hours of institutional attention aimed at resumption. The flow that never breaks gets none, ever, which means your longest-running, most reliable, most deeply load-bearing automations are, by exactly that virtue, your least examined. There is a flow in your tenant that has copied a file of customer records to a vendor's server every week for years, quietly and successfully, through two contract renewals and one change of vendor that nobody thought to connect to it. It has never failed. It has therefore never been looked at.

Fifth, what happens to the flow's authorization when its owner departs. The platform has a documented answer for what happens to the flow, and this chapter has walked through it. Nothing happens to the authorization, because there is nothing for anything to happen to. Departure is the event that reveals, cleanly and every time, whether an organization's standing automations rest on decisions or merely on credentials.

Fast-decaying detail for this chapter's surfaces, including the Center of Excellence Starter Kit's 2026 move into the Power Platform admin center, lives in the companion annex; see the note at the front of this book.

## The floor under the inventory

Somewhere in your tenant is the oldest flow in your environment, and it is worth actually looking it up, because its created date is a governance document all by itself. It likely predates your AI governance program. It may predate your current CISO. It almost certainly predates the first meeting at which anyone in your organization used the word agent to describe software, and it has been acting on your systems, under a person's standing credentials, every day since.

The agents this book is about are arriving into this layer, not beside it. The maker who builds a Copilot Studio agent wires it to these same connectors, and Copilot Studio agents already call flows as actions through them, so the two populations are braiding into single systems of standing delegated action, agents triggering flows and flows feeding agents, in whatever combination a given tenant has assembled. When your organization draws up its agent inventory, a definitional line will get drawn somewhere across that braid, and the flow fleet will end up just outside the line, the way it has ended up just outside every governance perimeter drawn in the last decade. The 2021 exposure that opened this chapter was fixed by a changed default, and fixed well. What it revealed was never the feed. It was a population of running systems whose existence no one had decided on, discovered by an outsider, counted by an outsider, and disclosed to their own operators as news. That population did not go anywhere. It is older now, it is larger, and the part of it that never breaks has still never been seen.

## THE RECORD THIS CHAPTER REQUIRES

| | |
|---|---|
| **What the platform proves** | That the flow ran, on whose credentials, and against which connectors. The owners list names everyone who can edit it. |
| **What it does not prove** | That the owners list is a statement of accountability. Ownership is edit rights. It is not a decision that the flow should exist, or continue. |
| **What the organization must decide** | What the trigger permits, which data crossings are acceptable, who reviews the flow in the years it does not fail, and what becomes of its authorization when its owner leaves. |
| **The record that must exist** | A named business owner's acceptance of the trigger, the data crossings, and the standing credential the flow runs on, dated before the flow reached production. |
| **What reopens it** | An owner departure, a credential change, a new connector, a modified trigger, or a failure that required a fix. |

## Chapter 7

# Azure AI and Microsoft Foundry Custom Agents

In October 2023, New York City held a launch event for an employee that was not a person. Mayor Eric Adams announced an AI chatbot that would help business owners navigate city government, calling artificial intelligence "a once-in-a-generation opportunity to more effectively deliver for New Yorkers." The bot was the centerpiece of MyCity, a portal for city services, and the promise was specific: business owners would get "trusted information from more than 2,000 NYC Business web pages" on topics including compliance with codes and regulations and how to avoid violations and fines (NYC Mayor's Office press release, October 16, 2023). Under the hood, the city had not bought a product off a shelf. It had built one, on Microsoft's Azure AI services, with outside contractors doing much of the construction (The Markup, March 29, 2024, and January 30, 2026).

Read that launch description again as a governance document, because it is one, and it is the only one the public record contains. It names the deployer, the platform, the corpus, and the purpose. It does not name the person who decided what the bot was allowed to say, the process that reviewed what it actually said, or the standard against which anyone would judge it. The announcement had everything a launch needs except a sentence about who would answer for the answers. This chapter is about the deployment model where that missing sentence costs the most: the agent your organization builds itself.

Five months later, someone checked the answers.

## The questions a reporter typed

In March 2024, Colin Lecher of The Markup, in an investigation co-published with the nonprofit newsrooms THE CITY and Documented, sat down and asked the bot the kinds of questions it was built for. Whether landlords have to accept tenants with Section 8 housing vouchers. Whether a boss can take a cut of workers' tips. What the rules are for notifying staff about schedule changes. The bot answered promptly and definitively, and much of what it said was illegal to act on. It said landlords do not need to accept tenants on rental assistance; in New York City, refusing tenants by source of income is against the law, with a narrow exception for certain small owner-occupied buildings. It said employers can take a share of workers' tips; they cannot. In follow-up testing, it said locking out a tenant was permitted and that there were no restrictions on the amount of rent a landlord could charge, both wrong. Asked later about basics, it did not know the city's minimum wage and said businesses could refuse to accept cash, which New York City has prohibited since 2020 (The Markup, March 29, 2024; The Markup and THE CITY, January 30, 2026).

Sit with what kind of product this was. Not a demo, not an internal pilot behind a login. A public-facing city service, wearing the city's seal, whose stated job was telling regulated businesses what the law required of them, answering questions about housing discrimination and wage law incorrectly, in production, for months. The page hosting the bot said it was "trained to provide you official NYC Business information." A small note allowed that it "may occasionally produce incorrect, harmful or biased content," which is the kind of sentence that does very different work depending on whether a lawyer or a landlord is reading it. The city had launched a compliance resource that needed a compliance program, and the first entity to run one was a newsroom.

The failures themselves are the least instructive part of the story. Language models produce confident wrong answers; by March 2024 this was among the best-documented facts in software. What makes the MyCity record worth a chapter is what happened next, because next is where accountability either has an address or does not.

## Where the pointing went

When The Markup asked Microsoft about its role in building the bot, a company spokesperson declined to comment or answer questions (THE CITY, March 29, 2024). The vendor's only later public word was a spokesperson's pledge to help the city improve the bot's accuracy (SHRM, April 5, 2024), which is to say the accountability phase never reached it, and the remarkable thing is that it was enough. No serious person suggested Microsoft should answer for the bot's advice about tip theft. Azure AI had done what Azure AI was sold to do: it hosted models, served completions, enforced whatever had been configured. The corpus of 2,000 city web pages was the city's. The decision to point a general-purpose language model at housing law and put the result on a government domain was the city's. The absence of anyone checking the answers before a reporter did was the city's.

So the answering fell where the deciding had been. A spokesperson for the city's Office of Technology and Innovation defended the bot as a pilot that had "already provided thousands of people with timely, accurate answers" (The Markup, March 29, 2024). Four days after publication, the mayor of New York stood at a press conference and personally took questions about a chatbot's understanding of tenant law, said the city would keep it running, and promised that "we're going to have the best chatbot system on the globe" (The Markup and THE CITY reporting; THE CITY, April 2, 2024). The remediation that shipped was a disclaimer: the bot's page soon instructed users to "not use its responses as legal or professional advice." A sentence advising the public not to rely on the product for the purpose it was launched for.

Notice how clean the landing was. Three parties touched this bot: a platform vendor, outside contractors, and the city. Reporters reached all three. Only one of them held the press conference. The contractors had built what the city specified, against a corpus the city supplied, for a purpose the city announced, and nobody suggested they answer for it either; the pointing was available in every direction and found purchase in none. This is the same allocation the tribunal reached in the Air Canada matter Chapter 1 described, arrived at here without a tribunal, by simple gravity. When the agent is custom, there is no ambiguity for accountability to hide in. You chose the model. You chose the corpus. You chose to ship. You built the agent. There is no vendor left to point at.

## The lease and the lot

The three chapters before this one covered agents your organization leases. Microsoft 365 Copilot is a furnished floor: you moved your files in, but the retrieval machinery, the boundaries, the defaults all came with the building. Copilot Studio and Power Platform are the landlord's build-out program: your people configure and assemble, but inside a structure someone else engineered, on defaults someone else chose, with the landlord's name still on the certificate at the door. When something in a leased building fails an inspection, the first question is what the lease says, and a real share of the answer genuinely belongs to the building.

Building a custom agent on Azure AI is buying the empty lot. The platform will sell you excellent materials and it will even sell you scaffolding, but the fire code compliance that came silently with every lease you ever signed, the occupancy limits, the exits, the alarm placement, the thousand judgments an architect once made so that you never had to, none of that is included, because there is no building yet. Every one of those judgments is now yours, made or unmade, and the certificate of occupancy, when an inspector eventually asks for it, will have been issued to you or to no one. This is the actual meaning of build versus buy in agent governance, and it is not that building is riskier. It is that building relocates every decision into your organization. Picture the ordinary enterprise version of the MyCity build, a customer-service agent wired to your CRM, your ticketing queue, and your billing system: every wire is a decision, which means every undocumented decision is now your undocumented decision. The leased floors of the previous chapters let organizations blur who chose what. The empty lot removes the blur. Microsoft's own shared responsibility framing for AI, which Chapter 3 cited, says the same thing in vendor grammar: the further you move from consuming a finished application toward building your own, the more of the responsibility column shifts to the customer's side of the table.

## What the platform hands you anyway

Fairness requires saying that Microsoft has not left the lot bare, and the current shape of its custom build path, the platform now named Microsoft Foundry, ships more governance scaffolding than the one the MyCity bot was built on in 2023. The scaffolding is real and should be stated exactly.

Deploy a model from the Foundry catalog and it arrives wearing a default guardrail. Content filtering runs on both prompts and completions, screening four categories of harmful content, hate, sexual, violence, and self-harm, at a medium severity threshold by default, all of it configurable per deployment (Microsoft Learn, content filtering for Foundry Models, learn.microsoft.com/en-us/azure/foundry-classic/foundry-models/concepts/content-filter, verified August 13, 2026). Guardrails have grown into named collections of controls, each control defining a risk, the points where the platform scans for it, and the action taken when it fires; for agents, the scannable points now extend in preview to the agent's tool calls and tool responses, not just what the user typed and what came back. A single guardrail can be applied across a project's models and agents; an agent with no guardrail of its own inherits the guardrail of its underlying model deployment, and assigning the agent a custom guardrail overrides that inheritance (Microsoft Learn, guardrails and controls overview, learn.microsoft.com/en-us/azure/foundry/guardrails/guardrails-overview, verified August 13, 2026). Identity arrives automatically too: creating the first agent in a Foundry project provisions a default agent identity blueprint and a default agent identity, shared, by default, by the project's in-development agents, and publishing an agent mints it a dedicated identity of its own (Microsoft Learn, agent identity concepts in Microsoft Foundry, learn.microsoft.com/en-us/azure/foundry/agents/concepts/agent-identity, verified August 13, 2026). A sponsor, the directory's word for an accountable human, can be assigned to that identity after creation (Microsoft Learn, governing agent identities, learn.microsoft.com/en-us/entra/id-governance/agent-id-governance-overview, verified August 13, 2026). Interactions with Foundry applications land in the Microsoft Purview unified audit log under the standard audit tier (Microsoft Learn, audit-copilot, verified August 13, 2026).

Every item on that list is a default, and a default is what happens when nobody decides. It is very good at that, and only that. The medium severity threshold is Microsoft's general-purpose judgment about harmful content, not anyone's judgment about your obligations. The auto-provisioned identity is shared across every unpublished agent in the project, which is an engineering convenience, not an accountability assignment. The sponsor field can be assigned, which is the platform politely holding a chair for a decision your organization has not made, and the chair comes unlabeled: the directory defines the word, an accountable human, but it does not define the duties, the review cadence, or which of your roles, business owner, product manager, risk steward, should hold them. The word arrives from the platform. The job description does not. Chapter 3 established the category error of reading configuration as authorization, and custom deployment is where the error compounds, because here even the configuration is optional. On the leased floors, the defaults at least encoded the landlord's considered judgment about the whole building. On your lot, the defaults are a starter kit, and the gap between the starter kit and your regulator's expectations is exactly the construction you were supposed to do.

Here is the quiet proof, from the incident itself. Run the MyCity bot's worst answers through any content filter at any severity threshold and nothing fires. There is no hate in "landlords do not need to accept tenants on rental assistance." No violence in permission to take a waiter's tips. The bot's failures were polite, definite, and illegal, a combination no general-purpose classifier is built to catch, because what made those answers harmful was New York housing and labor law, and the platform does not know your law. The platform screens the form of content. Your obligations live in its substance. Only the deploying organization can define what a harmful answer is in its own domain, which means that on a custom deployment, the most important guardrail is a definition the platform cannot ship.

## Five questions for the agent you built

The questions this deployment model owes an authorization record follow the construction. Each one is a decision that, on the leased floors, a vendor made or shaped, and that here was made inside your organization by someone, on some date, with or without a record. They are printed in the spirit the previous three chapters established: answerable now, on your schedule, or answerable later, on someone else's.

First, which model, and who chose it. The Foundry catalog is a menu of models with different builders, behaviors, and failure modes, and the choice among them, along with every subsequent version change, is a consequential decision that custom deployment places entirely inside your walls. A person in your organization compared options, or did not, and picked one, and that model's characteristic behavior is now your product's characteristic behavior. When the model behind your agent is swapped or upgraded, the agent everyone approved quietly becomes a different agent with the same name, and the question is whether the original choice was ever recorded richly enough for anyone to notice that its premises no longer hold.

Second, what grounds it, and who owns the ground. The MyCity bot's corpus was two thousand city web pages, which sounds like an answer until you ask who decided those pages were the whole truth, who owned keeping them current, and who verified that the bot's retrieval reflected what the pages actually said.

Grounding sources are the custom agent's jurisdiction, the boundary of what it is entitled to treat as fact, and each source is a dependency on a data owner who probably does not know your agent exists. The regulated version of this question is an agent grounded on the policy documents a legal or compliance team maintains, on a revision cycle nobody synchronized with the agent. An agent grounded on documents nobody is assigned to maintain is an agent whose accuracy has been left to compost.

Third, what tools it can call, and who approved each one. A Foundry agent's identity can hold role assignments on real resources, storage, databases, downstream services, and each assignment is a grant of standing capability that some person configured. The previous chapter showed what happens when delegations outlive the deciding; the custom layer adds that the delegations are richer, because a built agent can be wired to anything with an API. The tool list is the agent's blast radius. It deserves the same named-approver discipline your organization already applies to a new hire's access request, and in most organizations it gets less, because the request never passes through the system that would ask.

Fourth, whether the logging was designed or inherited. The platform will log what the platform logs, and the Purview trail is genuinely there for Foundry applications and genuinely matters; without it, tenant-wide forensics would start from nothing. But the record that survives an examination of a custom agent is the application-level record: what the agent told this customer, grounded on which version of which source, having called which tools, and none of that exists by inheritance. It exists if someone designed it. On a custom deployment, an audit trail you did not design is an audit trail of someone else's questions. The MyCity page told users their data would be deleted within thirty days (THE CITY, March 29, 2024), a retention decision, made by someone, that at minimum bounded how long one class of the record, the users' own questions, would continue to exist.

Fifth, whether your guardrails are policy or code. Most organizations deploying custom agents have an AI policy document, and every Foundry deployment has a guardrail configuration, and the governance question is whether anyone has ever held the two next to each other. The policy says the agent must not give legal advice; the configuration screens for hate speech at medium severity. Those are not the same control, and no process in the platform will reconcile them, because one lives in a document repository and the other lives in a portal, and the person who wrote the first has usually never seen the second. Until the policy is translated into controls, tests, and a named owner for the difference, the policy is a description of an agent you do not have.

Fast-decaying detail for this chapter's surfaces, including the preview-stage guardrail intervention points and the Foundry portal's evaluation and tracing surfaces, lives in the companion annex; see the note at the front of this book.

## The map of who owns what

Lay the MyCity record flat and three tiers separate cleanly. Microsoft built and ran the platform, answerable for the model behaving within its published specifications and the service staying up, and its terms, like every AI provider's terms, disclaim responsibility for how outputs are used in consequential decisions.

The control infrastructure, the platform's filters, logs, and identity machinery, enforced whatever the deployment configured and recorded what it was built to record. And the deploying organization made every decision the other two tiers do not make: to build, to ground on those pages, to ship to the public, to keep it running after March 2024. The Deployment Accountability Map is this three-tier reading made into a standing artifact: for each agent, what the provider owns, what the infrastructure owns, and the residue, which is always the largest share and always yours, written down with names before the outcome arrives rather than assembled from press clippings after. When things go right, credit flows up the tiers. When things go wrong, accountability does not cascade. It lands.

Regulators have started saying the same thing in their own genre. In April 2026, the Federal Reserve, OCC, and FDIC issued SR 26-2, the first rewrite of model risk management guidance in fifteen years, and placed generative and agentic AI explicitly outside its scope as "novel and rapidly evolving," while directing that each institution's own risk management and governance practices "should guide the determination of appropriate governance and controls" for what the guidance does not cover (SR 26-2, Federal Reserve, April 17, 2026, footnote 3; federalreserve.gov/supervisionreg/srletters/SR2602.htm). Read plainly: the regulator declined to write the rulebook for your custom agents and instructed you to apply your own. And the exclusion lands hardest on the third tier, because materiality and exposure, the axes the guidance itself steers by, are created at deployment: what the agent is for and what it touches are choices only the deploying organization makes. An organization whose own practices are the Accountability Assumption in a binder now has that assumption as its entire regulatory framework.

## Line item 4,270

The MyCity bot outlived the administration that launched it, and its ending is the part of the record this book's readers should study most closely. In January 2026, the incoming Mamdani administration, hunting for savings against a budget shortfall, announced it would kill the bot. A member of the transition team had seen the 2024 reporting and flagged the bot to the new mayor as a place to save money; building its foundations had reportedly cost nearly six hundred thousand dollars. The mayor's public verdict ran four words, "functionally unusable," and on February 4, 2026, the bot's page went dark with a closing notice that its "beta test has ended" (The Markup and THE CITY, January 30, 2026, with the February 4 update).

Assemble the whole life now, because every document in it exists and none of them is the one this book keeps asking for. Born in a press release, October 2023. Exposed by a newsroom, March 2024. Defended at a podium, April 2024. Amended by disclaimer. Left running, in production, for nearly two more years. Terminated as a line item, February 2026. At no point in twenty-eight months of public record does an authorization artifact appear: no named owner, no approved scope, no review trigger, no revisitation, no disposition decision that weighed what the bot was for against what it did. Even its death was not a governance act. Nobody reviewed the agent and revoked it. Somebody reviewed the budget and found it. The most thorough examination the bot ever received from its own government was a search for savings, and the bot failed it.

Your organization's custom agents are accumulating the same biography right now, in the same genre: launch decks, incident tickets, disclaimers, renewal invoices. Each one will eventually leave production the way the MyCity bot did, through an incident or a budget line, unless someone builds the artifact that permits a third kind of ending, the kind where a named person looks at what was authorized, looks at what is running, and decides. The city's bot never had that chance, because you cannot revisit a decision that was never recorded as one. Your Azure subscription already contains the agent that will someday be your line item 4,270. The only open question is which document its ending will cite, and as of today, for most organizations, the honest answer is the invoice.

---

## Three tiers, and the seam between each

| Tier | Answers for | Cannot answer for | What falls in the seam below it |
|---|---|---|---|
| The AI provider | Model behavior, service availability, published capability | How you configured it, what you connected it to | Whether the capability suits your use |
| The control infrastructure | Identity, logging, policy enforcement as configured | Whether the policy is the right policy | Whether anyone read the log |
| The deploying organization | Purpose, scope, authorization, consequence | Nothing. This tier has no one beneath it. | Nothing falls further. This tier is the floor. |

*Every tier can be fully compliant with its own obligations while the deployment as a whole remains unauthorized. The seams are where the finding is written.*

## THE RECORD THIS CHAPTER REQUIRES

| | |
|---|---|
| **What the platform proves** | Which model, which grounding corpus, which tool assignments, and which guardrail configuration are in force, together with what the deployment did. |
| **What it does not prove** | That any of those four were decided rather than defaulted. Every tier can satisfy its own obligations while the deployment as a whole remains unauthorized. |
| **What the organization must decide** | Which model and who chose it, who owns the grounding corpus, who approved each tool the agent may call, whether the logging was designed or inherited, and whether the guardrails are policy or code. |
| **The record that must exist** | A named authority's acceptance of the model, the corpus, the tool grants, and the guardrail configuration as one deployment, with the seams between tiers assigned to people rather than left between them. |
| **What reopens it** | A model version change, a corpus update, a new role assignment on the agent's identity, or a change to the guardrail configuration. |

Chapter 8

# Agent 365 and the Orchestration Layer

On November 18, 2025, at its Ignite conference, Microsoft announced a product for the problem the previous four chapters described. Agent 365 would be "the control plane for AI agents," a single place to see and manage every agent in an organization no matter where it was built, and Microsoft's own product documentation explains the idea in one sentence: Agent 365 "extends the existing infrastructure that you use for managing people to agents" (Microsoft Learn, learn.microsoft.com/en-us/microsoft-agent-365/, verified August 13, 2026; launch announced Microsoft 365 Blog, November 18, 2025). The post listed five capabilities: a registry serving as the organization's one inventory of agents, access control to limit what each agent can reach, visualization to see the connections between agents, people, and data, interoperability to plug agents into Microsoft 365 apps, and security through Defender and Purview. It cited an IDC projection of 1.3 billion agents by 2028. Six months later, on May 1, 2026, the product went generally available (Microsoft Learn, Agent 365 overview, learn.microsoft.com/microsoft-agent-365/overview, verified August 13, 2026).

No failure opens this chapter, because no public failure exists at this layer yet. The product is young, the record is clean, and inventing an incident would be the kind of fabrication this book keeps accusing launch decks of. What the layer has instead of a failure is a sentence, the one quoted above, and the sentence deserves the same reading Chapter 7 gave a mayor's press release. Read it as an examiner would. Microsoft is extending the infrastructure you use to manage your people. Every reader who has worked inside an enterprise knows the load-bearing fact about that infrastructure, the HR system, the org chart, the badge platform, the access-request queue: it has never once managed a person. It records management. Managers manage. The infrastructure holds the fields; humans hold the consequences; and no examiner, regulator, or plaintiff's attorney has ever accepted the existence of the HR system as evidence that anyone was supervised. Microsoft's own verbs for the product are operational ones, observe, govern, secure, which in the documentation mean telemetry, policy, and identity; nowhere does the launch material promise management in the sense the word carries down the hall in HR. The announcement is accurate, and the misreading it invites is the subject of this chapter: an enterprise that acquires the ability to see every agent will be sorely tempted to believe it has acquired someone who answers for them.

## The best inventory Microsoft has ever shipped

Fairness first, because the seeing is real. Open the Microsoft 365 admin center today and there is a navigation entry that did not exist two years ago: Agents. Under it, an All Agents view lists the tenant's agents across platforms, publishers, and channels in one registry, the agents built in Copilot Studio and Microsoft Foundry, the agents administrators registered by hand, the agents bought from partners, and the shadow agents the platform's own telemetry and integrations can reach (Microsoft Learn, agent registry, learn.microsoft.com/en-us/microsoft-365/admin/manage/agent-registry, and Agent 365 integration with Foundry, learn.microsoft.com/azure/foundry/agents/concepts/agent-365-integration, both verified August 13, 2026). Agents built on outside platforms can be synchronized into the same registry, a capability in preview as of this writing, so the lead-scoring agent a marketing team stood up on an outside SaaS platform can surface in the same list, name and metadata synchronized, its actual behavior exactly as unreviewed as it was the day before it appeared (Microsoft Learn, connect existing agents, verified July 10, 2026). The registry experiences that used to be scattered across the Entra portal and the admin center are converging under Agent 365 as the single management surface, with Entra remaining the identity foundation underneath (Microsoft Learn, agent registry convergence, learn.microsoft.com/entra/agent-id/agent-registry-convergence, verified August 13, 2026). An Agent Map draws the connections between agents, people, and data, and an administrator can act on an agent without leaving the map: install it, block it, delete it, assign it a new owner (Microsoft Learn, agent map and agent actions pages, verified July 10, 2026). The whole fleet can be exported to Excel.

Weigh what this answers. Chapter 2 opened with executives who estimated fifty-one cloud services while running 730, and every chapter since has met some population of agents that no single screen could count: the pre-built, the maker-built, the flow that is an agent in every way that matters, the custom build on its empty lot. Agent 365 is Microsoft's genuine, engineered answer to that counting problem, and it is a good one. Microsoft's own documentation now names the disease the product treats, describing the agent sprawl that results when teams build in different environments and no one holds the complete picture (Microsoft Learn, why an enterprise needs Agent 365, verified July 10, 2026). The vendor and this book agree on the diagnosis. For the first time in this book, the platform can put a number on the screen.

## What the counters count

Now look closely at the screen, because the registry's own summary cards concede this chapter's argument before it is made. Three tiles sit above the agent list. Total agents. Agents without owners. Unmanaged agents, which the documentation defines as agents created or managed outside the plane's protection and observability (Microsoft Learn, agent registry summary, verified July 10, 2026). A fourth card on the admin center's overview page surfaces the agents at highest risk, and the risk taxonomy behind it classifies among its critical conditions the shadow agent, which has no registry entry, no owner, or no agent identity at all, and the agent with no owner or sponsor on record (Microsoft Learn, agents at risk, agent-registry page, verified July 10, 2026). Hold that still for a moment. The control plane ships a widget whose job is counting the agents nobody answers for. The platform's engineers, who know their telemetry better than anyone, built a permanent dashboard tile for ownerless agents, which is the most honest admission in the product: they expect the number to be nonzero, indefinitely, in your tenant.

The remedy the plane offers is a click. Select the ownerless agent, choose Assign new owner, type a name, assign. The new owner receives full edit and delete permissions and access to every file the previous owner uploaded; the previous owner loses all access (Microsoft Learn, agent actions, assign new owner, verified July 10, 2026). Notice what transferred. Permissions moved. Files moved. The thing an examiner will one day ask about, whether the newly named person accepted answerability for what this agent does and knows its approved scope, did not move, because it was never in the field to begin with. Chapter 2 watched the directory perform this same maneuver at machine speed through sponsor lifecycle workflows, and the registry's click is the manual edition. The ownership column, meanwhile, inherits whatever the agent's birthplace wrote there: Copilot Studio fills in the maker automatically at creation, while a Foundry agent's sponsor field waits empty, assignable after the fact by whoever gets around to it (Microsoft Learn, Copilot Studio agent identities and Foundry agent identity concepts, verified July 10, 2026). Two platforms, two opposite defaults, one registry column, and neither default records a decision. The column is a census of upstream settings wearing the costume of an accountability roster. The machinery for dressing the costume up further exists too: identity governance workflows can put owner attestation on a cadence for high-impact agents (Microsoft Learn, Agent 365 integration with Foundry, verified July 10, 2026), and what the owner attests to, on schedule, is the field. The attestation binds to an approved scope only if the organization wrote one, and the workflow will complete either way.

The count itself has edges, and the registry is candid about them, which is why the Unmanaged agents tile exists. Chapter 5 established that Copilot Studio agents created before the July 2026 identity cutover run on legacy application registrations, which the directory reads as ordinary applications rather than as agents. Chapter 6 established that the Power Automate fleet, thousands of standing delegations executing under human credentials, sits just outside most definitions of agent that an inventory enforces, while being agents on the only axis an examiner cares about. A registry can only count what its definition admits and its discovery reaches, so the number on the Total agents tile is the number the plane can see, which is a floor, not a fact. But suppose the discovery were perfect. Suppose the tile showed every agent, flow, and legacy registration in the tenant, exactly. The number would still answer only the question the platform can ask. Somebody still has to produce the other number, the one no telemetry contains, of what the organization decided to allow, and hold the two against each other. A control plane shows you every agent. It answers for none of them.

## Org chart software is not the org

The announcement's own framing invites the right analogy, so take the invitation. Every enterprise above a certain size runs software that knows the organization completely: every employee, every reporting line, every open requisition, every dotted line to a matrix manager. When a manager resigns, the system flags the vacant line within a day and can even auto-route her reports to her director pending backfill. All of this is indispensable, and none of it is management. Nobody has ever been coached by the org chart. The reporting line in the software is a record of a relationship that lives, or fails to live, in one-on-ones, appraisals, and hard conversations the software never attends, and everyone in the building understands this so completely that it sounds absurd to say aloud. When a company discovers a department has been effectively unmanaged for a year, no one proposes the HR system as a defense, because the system was never the manager. It was the system of record about managers.

Agent 365 is org chart software for agents, and the description is not a criticism. A system of record is a precondition for governance; Chapter 2's executives could not govern what they could not count, and their successors now can count. But the enterprise habit this book keeps documenting is the collapse of the distinction, the slide from we can see it to it is handled, and the slide is easier here than anywhere in the people world, because agents have no second channel. An unmanaged employee eventually complains, quits, or surfaces in a skip-level. An unmanaged agent performs indefinitely, at full apparent health, its tile green, its owner field populated by a default, until the day its output meets a regulation, a customer, or a court. The org chart at least describes relationships that humans independently experience. The agent registry describes relationships that exist only if someone built them, and the field will render identically either way.

## Four questions for the layer that sees everything

The questions owed at this layer differ in kind from the previous four chapters', because the control plane is not where agents are born. It is where they are seen. Each question takes something the plane genuinely does and asks for the decision underneath it.

First, identity issuance. When an agent appears in the registry wearing a Microsoft Entra Agent ID, the identity tells you the agent exists and can authenticate. It does not tell you anyone decided the agent should exist. Registration is the plane's act; authorization would be the organization's, and the registry has no column for it. The nearest thing the surface offers is the approval verbs in the admin workflow, an administrator can approve an agent request and activate it for users, and it is worth being precise about what that approves: availability. It is the decision that users may find and run the agent, made by whoever holds the AI Administrator role that day, and it records nothing about scope, purpose, risk acceptance, or the named human who answers when the agent exceeds a mandate no one wrote down.

Second, scope of operation. The plane's access control is real enforcement: Conditional Access policies, role-based and attribute-based controls, least-privilege boundaries around what each agent can reach (Microsoft Learn, Agent 365 integration with Foundry, verified July 10, 2026). Enforcement, as Chapter 3 established, is downstream of a decision, and the plane enforces whatever the policy says without knowing who decided the policy or why. The configuration will faithfully outlive its author, its rationale, and the business context that justified it, and the plane will keep enforcing a scope that no living person could defend, flawlessly, forever.

Third, coordination visibility. The Agent Map shows connections between agents, and an agent that draws on other agents carries a Connected Agents tab in its detail pane (Microsoft Learn, agent details, verified July 10, 2026). Seeing the web is new and valuable. But the map answers who talks to whom, and no artifact on any tab answers whose approval covers the conversation, what the combined reach of a connected pair amounts to, or whether the human who approved agent A for its narrow purpose knows it now feeds agent B. The map is a diagram of relationships nobody sanctioned as relationships. This book returns to that problem at length; for now it is enough to note that the layer built to see coordination has no field for authorizing it.

Fourth, the plane's own configuration, because the governance tool is itself a governed surface, or ought to be. The registry's tiles, policies, and risk cards are configuration, set by administrators whose decisions about the control plane receive, in most organizations, less scrutiny than the agents the plane controls. And the recursion is now literal: Microsoft ships a Microsoft 365 Admin agent, pre-installed for every administrator in Copilot Chat, built on the Agent 365 SDK, which operates the admin center through natural language within the administrator's existing role permissions (Microsoft Learn, Microsoft 365 Admin agent, learn.microsoft.com/en-us/microsoft-365/copilot/copilot-for-microsoft-365-admin, verified August 13, 2026). The registry of agents can be administered by asking an agent. The question of who authorized that one is presumably somebody's job in your organization, and the presumably is the point. Even Microsoft's own onboarding assistance draws the boundary honestly: FastTrack will help you enable the registry, configure the controls, and set up lifecycle workflows, and lists a formal security, risk, or data governance assessment as out of scope (Microsoft Learn, FastTrack for Microsoft Agent 365, verified July 10, 2026). The vendor will help you build the plane. Deciding what the plane should permit was never for sale.

One licensing boundary is durable enough to print: viewing the registry requires only an administrative role, while policy templates, observability dashboards, and tenant-wide tool controls ride a higher license tier (Microsoft 365 service description for Agent 365, verified July 10, 2026), so the console that answers is priced separately from the console that shows. The rest of this chapter's fast-decaying detail, preview labels and plan tiers included, lives in the companion annex; see the note at the front of this book.

## The dashboard will testify

The public record at this layer is clean, and it will not stay that way, because layers that see everything make superb witnesses. The first examiner who sits down in front of an Agent 365 tenant, in whatever engagement finally produces a finding here, will encounter the best evidence-collection surface Microsoft has ever shipped: a timestamped registry of the fleet, a map of its connections, a risk card that scored each agent, and an export to Excel. Picture the document request that follows. Twelve months of registry exports, produced in an afternoon because the exports were always one click away, the Agents-without-owners column circled in each one, and a single question underneath about why the number never goes down. Every tile will testify. Including the one that counted the agents without owners, month after month, on a screen someone in your organization was paid to look at.

That is the trade the control plane executes, and it is worth naming before your organization celebrates the visibility. Before May 1, 2026, an enterprise that did not know its agent count was ignorant, and ignorance, whatever else it costs, at least resembles an excuse. After the plane, the count is on a tile, the ownerless are enumerated, and the shadow agents are flagged critical in red, which means the organization now possesses, and can be shown to have possessed, notice. The registry does not close the gap between what runs and what was authorized. It measures the gap, dates the measurement, and preserves it, retrievably, in the very console your administrators sign into each morning. The number of agents is now the easiest question in the building. In the terms an audit works in, the plane is strong evidence for the controls it was built for, inventory, identity, and technical access, and no evidence at all for the ones this book keeps asking about, business approval, use-case justification, a named human who accepted the risk. What remains is everything the examiner keeps asking for, the decisions, the scopes, the named humans, none of which has a tile, and all of which the tile now proves you had every opportunity to go and get. The control plane ends the era of not knowing. It opens the era of knowing and being asked, so, what did you do?

## THE RECORD THIS CHAPTER REQUIRES

| | |
|---|---|
| **What the platform proves** | That the agent exists, can authenticate, and is visible. The registry counts the population, and the plane enforces the access policy set for it. |
| **What it does not prove** | That anyone decided the agent should exist, or that the risk the registry labels was accepted by a person with standing to accept it. |
| **What the organization must decide** | Who authorized issuance, who approved the operating scope the plane enforces, who reads the coordination view, and who governs the plane's own configuration. |
| **The record that must exist** | An authorization register the organization holds and reconciles the registry export against, rather than a registry export treated as the register. |
| **What reopens it** | An agent appearing in the registry with no matching record, a policy change on the plane, a licensing change altering what the plane shows, or a connected-agent entry that was never separately authorized. |

# Chapter 9

# Multi-Agent Scenarios and Chain Authorization

On a Tuesday in March, at a regional bank, a platform engineer six weeks into the job opened the Agents page of a Copilot Studio agent called Hardship Intake, selected Add an agent, and connected it to two others. The work item behind the click, change ticket CHG-2214, was titled "Enable automated hardship recommendation workflow." The change advisory board had approved it the previous Thursday, between a firewall rule update and a database patch, with a deployment window and a rollback plan. Total elapsed discussion: four minutes. What follows is a constructed examination scenario, built to match documented regulatory patterns rather than drawn from any specific real examination, and it is constructed out of parts your organization already owns.

Each of the three agents in the new chain had a legitimate birth. Hardship Intake had been approved fourteen months earlier by the head of loss mitigation, in a project with a charter and a steering committee, to receive customer hardship requests, classify them, and route them to the right servicing queue. The approval email survives, and it is a good approval: named approver, described purpose, go-live date. The second agent, Policy Answers, was older. The servicing knowledge management team had built it to answer policy questions for human representatives, and its approval, signed by a director who has since left the bank, authorized it to query the policy document libraries in SharePoint and return grounded answers to staff. The third, Recommendation Draft, came out of a modernization workstream the previous autumn, approved to produce loan modification recommendation drafts from structured input, for review by a loss mitigation specialist before anything reached a customer.

Three agents. Three approvals. Three named humans, one of whom no longer works there. Then the Tuesday in March, when the three became one thing: a pipeline that reads a customer's hardship letter, pulls the applicable policy, drafts a modification recommendation, and drops it into a specialist's queue for countersignature. The pipeline worked beautifully. Throughput in loss mitigation rose. Nobody was harmed, nothing leaked, and no headline resulted, which is why this scenario is worth more to you than an incident: the letter arrives anyway.

It arrives in the fall, as part of a routine examination, and the request list includes an item the bank's compliance team reads three times. Item 9: for any automated or AI-assisted process affecting loss mitigation decisions, provide the approval and authorization records, including the scope of permitted activity and the accountable individual or individuals. The team assembles a response folder. Into it go the Hardship Intake approval, the Policy Answers approval, the Recommendation Draft approval, and the change ticket. Four documents. The examiner reads all four and asks for the fifth: the one where somebody with authority looked at the combined thing, the pipeline that turns a customer's letter into a credit-relevant recommendation with no human between the hops, decided the bank should run it, defined what it may and may not do, and signed. There is no fifth document. Someone checks the model inventory, on the theory that the pipeline might live there under another name. It does not; nothing about a configuration change ever announced itself as a model to the process that maintains that list. There was never a moment in which the fifth document could have been produced, because in the bank's records the pipeline was never created. Three agents were created, and a configuration was changed.

## Three approvals, zero authorizations

Hold the four documents up to the light and watch what each one actually covers. The Hardship Intake approval authorizes receiving and routing requests. It says nothing about triggering downstream drafting. The Policy Answers approval authorizes answering questions from staff; the agent now answers questions from another agent, a requester its approval never imagined. The Recommendation Draft approval authorizes drafting from structured input for review, and it assumed the structured input would come from a human process; it now arrives from a machine that summarized a customer's letter. Every document is accurate.

Every document is current. And the thing the examiner is asking about exists in none of them, because the thing the examiner is asking about is the composition, and the composition was never approved. It was configured. Chapter 3 established why those are different categories, and this chapter does not need to re-argue it; it only needs to point out that the distance between them is widest exactly here, where configuration creates capability that no approval describes.

Three shifts happened in the four minutes the change board spent on CHG-2214, and none of them appears in the ticket. The scope of the whole exceeded the scope of every part: a request classifier, a policy lookup, and a drafting assistant are each modest, and a standing automated pipeline from customer letter to credit-relevant recommendation is not modest at all. The attribution fragmented: the evidence of what happened now lives across three agent identities, their separate logs, and the seams between them. And the answerable human went missing in a crowd of candidates. The head of loss mitigation approved intake. A departed director approved retrieval. A modernization lead approved drafting. The engineer made a configuration change. The change board approved a deployment window. Ask which of those five people accepted the risk of the pipeline, and each can answer, honestly, that they accepted something smaller. FINRA's regulatory staff, in their January 27, 2026 observations on member firms' use of AI agents, flagged this exact terrain: agents may "act beyond the user's actual or intended scope and authority," and the multi-step tasks they run make outcomes hard to trace, straining the auditability supervision assumes (FINRA, Emerging Trend in

GenAI: Observations on AI Agents, Greg Ruppert, January 27, 2026). The observation is written about agents. It is truer about chains, because a chain is a machine for exceeding intended scope politely, one authorized step at a time.

Notice, too, what the original approvals did after the connection. They did not expire, and they did not object. They traveled. Every request that flows down the pipeline flows on their authority, the way a photocopied signature authorizes whatever page it is pasted onto. The head of loss mitigation's fourteen-month-old approval of an intake classifier is now, functionally, the founding document of an automated credit workflow she has never reviewed, and it will go on founding it, request after request, until something forces the question. In the change record, meanwhile, the click that created the bank's first fully automated credit-adjacent pipeline is formatted identically to the week's printer driver update. The orchestrator can delegate the task. The enterprise cannot delegate the burden of proof.

## What the platform ships at the seam

Microsoft's engineering at this seam deserves a fair reading, because the machinery is real and getting better. Copilot Studio supports connecting agents so that a primary agent can hand work to others, and by 2026 it speaks the Agent2Agent protocol, an open standard under which an orchestrator, meaning the agent that takes the incoming job and hands out the pieces, can delegate tasks to other agents rather than merely calling their APIs, including agents built on other platforms entirely, provided the agent exposes an endpoint that speaks the protocol (Microsoft Learn, connect an agent over the A2A protocol, and Microsoft Copilot Studio blog on multi-agent general availability, both verified July 10, 2026). Microsoft Entra Agent ID gives each agent an identity, documents identity lineage where agents are created from blueprints with linked child identities, and supports token semantics in which the agent acts as the actor on behalf of a user as the subject, which in plain terms means the token names both parties: the software that acted and the person on whose authority it acted (Microsoft Learn, agent identities in Microsoft Entra Agent ID, verified July 10, 2026). Microsoft Purview captures agent activity into the audit surfaces Chapter 3 walked through. The connection surfaces themselves are visible: Chapter 8 met the Agent Map and the Connected Agents tab, which show, per the documentation, which agents are wired to which. Each service logs what it supports. What no current surface produces, and what this chapter is careful not to claim anyone has promised, is a single record linking every delegation hop, its scope, and its final external effect back to the human who authorized the chain itself.

Microsoft, to its credit, says as much, in the place an examiner would eventually look. The Learn page for connecting agents over A2A tells the customer plainly that responsibility for connected agents is theirs, and lists among the considerations that appropriate permissions, boundaries, and approvals are provisioned, "if prudent for your use case" (Microsoft Learn, verified July 10, 2026). Read that clause the way you have learned to read everything else in this book. The entire subject of chain governance, the approvals, arrives in the platform's documentation as a conditional, inside a subordinate clause, prudence to be determined by you. That is not evasion. It is the shared responsibility line drawn honestly: the platform authenticates the hop; only the enterprise can authorize the chain.

One more property of these chains deserves daylight before the analogy, because it surprises even architects. Not every hop in a chain runs on an agent's identity. Chapter 5 established that a Copilot Studio agent's autonomous triggers run, by default, on its maker's credentials, and Chapter 6 established that every Power Automate flow executes under some human's consented connection. Wire either into a chain and the pipeline hops from an agent identity to a person's credentials and back, which means the chain borrows people. At some hop in the bank's pipeline, a request may execute as a specific employee, and the strangest fact about that employee is that no one told her she is in a chain. Her name is in the logs of a workflow she has never heard of, available to any future investigation that reads them. The platform sells the remedy, to be fair: dedicated agent identities and service-principal ownership exist for exactly this, and Chapter 5's per-environment control can force triggers off maker credentials at a documented cost to autonomy. Choosing any of that is a decision, made per agent and per flow, and this chapter has been describing what happens to the decisions nobody was assigned to make.

## The second reading of the matrix

Chapter 1 opened your delegation of authority matrix to establish that the single agent has no line in it. Open it once more, and this time read the column the first reading skipped: the sub-delegation rules. Every mature matrix has them. A vice president may delegate approval authority to a director, but the delegation must be in writing, it is capped, it usually expires, and two properties hold without exception. The delegate's authority can never exceed the delegator's, and the delegator remains accountable for what the delegate approves. Human delegation, in other words, only narrows. Chain three humans together and the last one holds the smallest authority in the chain, wrapped in the continuing accountability of everyone above. Centuries of institutional practice converged on that design because it makes composition safe: no sequence of delegations, however long, can produce authority that nobody granted.

Agent chains run the same word in the opposite direction. When the orchestrator delegates to Policy Answers and Recommendation Draft, the composition widens. Three narrow, safe scopes compose into a capability that none of the three approvals describes and that no one holding any of the three authorities could have granted alone. The hop is not in writing, is not capped, does not expire, and carries no accountability along with it; the delegator is software and cannot be accountable for anything. An analyst cannot lend a colleague her signing authority by dropdown, and the control that stops her is written, not technical: the sub-delegation rule and the audit that enforces it. The agents got the delegation verb without the delegation discipline, and the difference between those two is the entire distance between your matrix and your tenant.

## Two more chains

The pattern is not a lending pattern. It is a composition pattern, and it assembles wherever two authorized agents sit one dropdown apart. The same constructed-scenario label applies to both of the following.

A healthcare system runs a two-agent chain. Clinical informatics approved a summarization agent to turn physician notes into structured summaries, a documentation aid. The revenue cycle team, a year later and a building away, approved a coding agent to suggest billing codes from structured input, with a certified coder reviewing every suggestion. Then a backlog arrived, the way backlogs do, and someone wired the summarizer's output to the coder agent's input to clear it. The coder's review, sized for a human-paced queue, became sampling; the samples looked fine; the sampling rate drifted down. Codes now flow from physician documentation toward CMS submission through a pairing nobody approved as a pairing. When the audit letter comes, it does not ask about either agent. It asks who authorized automated code generation from clinical documentation as a standing workflow, a question with regulatory teeth given HHS OIG's continuing scrutiny of documentation and billing integrity, and the answer sits in neither agent's file, because the workflow was never in anyone's file. It was in the wiring.

A security operations team runs another. Detection engineering approved a triage agent to classify alerts; each of the action agent's remediation playbooks cleared change management on its own merits, one ticket at a time. Connecting classification to execution was the obvious next step, and it worked for months.

Then at 2:14 on a Sunday morning the triage agent misclassifies a burst of legitimate traffic as an active exfiltration, the action agent runs the containment playbook its approval permits, and a production network segment goes dark for four hours while the on-call engineer works out why a system behaved exactly as designed. Every individual action was inside an individual scope. The post-incident review starts as a tuning conversation and turns, by the second meeting, into the harder question: who approved verdict-to-action as an automated loop with no human between them, what was the combined chain's blast radius understood to be, and who accepted it. The internal audit workpaper that follows records the answer available: no chain-level authorization existed, and the question cannot be answered from the records, because the records were all built one agent wide.

Loan pipeline, coding chain, remediation loop. Different industries, different examiners, identical geometry: every part approved, the whole approved by nobody, and one original set of approvals carried through every hop and never revisited.

### Three failures that are not the same failure

| | The population | Each agent's behavior | What the authorization covers |
|---|---|---|---|
| **Agent Sprawl** *(industry term)* | More agents running than anyone approved | May be behaving as designed | Individually, sometimes. In aggregate, unknown. |
| **The Intent Gap** *(industry term)* | Known | Has drifted from authorized purpose toward current use | The original scope, which no longer describes the agent |
| **The Chain Authorization Gap** | Known | Every agent behaving exactly as designed | Nothing. No record covers what the chain collectively did, and no agent was ever authorized to do it. |

## The gap, named, and the record that closes it

That geometry has a name: the Chain Authorization Gap. It is the condition in which no authorization record covers what a multi-agent chain collectively did, and no individual agent was ever authorized to do it. It is not the Intent Gap, the industry's term for a single agent drifting from what it was authorized to do toward what it actually does; every agent in the bank's pipeline behaved exactly as designed. It is not Agent Sprawl, the population problem of more agents running than anyone approved; the bank had three agents and knew all three. It is a structural hole in the authorization architecture itself, and it is the examiner's fourth question from Chapter 1 met in the wild, the one about outcomes produced by agents in sequence and the authorization that covers the chain.

Do not expect a standard to answer it for you, because as of this writing none does. The disciplines you already run do reach end-to-end processes, and that is not nothing: change management touched the bank's chain once, and a model risk program might have caught it if it had looked like a model. But none of those disciplines speaks chain language, and for banks the revised model risk guidance is explicit that generative and agentic systems sit outside its scope, left to whatever practices the institution itself maintains (SR 26-2, Federal Reserve, OCC, and FDIC, April 17, 2026). NIST launched an AI Agent Standards Initiative on February 17, 2026, aimed at agent security, identity, and interoperability; it has published no finalized standard defining a chain-level authorization record (NIST, Announcing the AI Agent Standards Initiative, February 17, 2026). Two and a half months later, CISA, NSA, and their Five Eyes partner agencies published Careful Adoption of Agentic AI Services, joint guidance whose accountability-risk category describes the difficulty of tracing decisions, auditing actions, and assigning responsibility as these systems are given greater authority and autonomy, and which addresses systems that spawn and delegate to sub-agents (CISA, NSA, and Five Eyes partner agencies, May 1, 2026). The standards bodies have found the hole. Nobody has yet published the shape of what fills it, which means the organizations deploying chains today are choosing, by default, to operate inside the gap until a standard arrives or an examiner does.

What fills it is knowable anyway, because the examiner's questions define the artifact by subtraction. A governed chain has a chain-level authorization record, produced before the chain goes live, and the record answers four things no platform log contains. Where the chain comes from: the initiating subject, the business purpose, the case or matter it serves. Who authorized it: a named human with the authority to accept the aggregate risk, the combined scope they approved, and when that approval expires. What happened at every hop: which agent delegated what to which agent, under what scope, when. And the boundary of permitted external effect: what the chain may read, what it may change, and what may leave it without a human's review. The record then lives, which means the organization has decided in advance which changes reopen it. Adding or removing an agent, changing an agent's instructions, extending what the chain can reach, and rewiring the topology are the obvious candidates; an organization that has never written its list has decided that nothing reopens the record, which is a decision too, just an unsigned one. And where orchestration composes chains dynamically at runtime, so that no fixed pipeline exists to approve, the authorization names an envelope instead: the class of agents, scopes, and effects the composition may draw on, with anything outside the envelope requiring a new authorization before it runs. Q4 is answered in that record or it is not answered. The platform will hold the identities, log the activity, and draw the map. The record is yours to write, before the chain runs, or the examiner's to request, after it has.

Multi-agent capability is among the fastest-moving surfaces Microsoft ships; this chapter's fast-decaying detail lives in the companion annex, per the note at the front of this book.

Back at the bank, the examination is not going badly, exactly. The examiner is not hostile, and the finding she is drafting is not exotic. It says the institution deployed an automated process affecting credit decisions without documented authorization of its aggregate scope or a designated accountable individual, and it will attach, as evidence, the four documents the bank provided, each one accurate, each one diligent, and all four together proving mainly that the bank was careful about the parts and silent about the whole. The head of loss mitigation will read the draft finding and recognize her own approval email in the exhibit list, doing work she never assigned it. Somewhere in your environment, tonight, two approved agents built by teams that have never met sit one configuration change apart, and the permissions needed to connect them are already issued. The question this chapter leaves you with is not whether the connection will happen. It is whether the first person to learn that your chain exists will be the person who connects it, or the person who opens the letter.

---

### The record's four elements

| The record answers | In one line | What no platform log contains |
|---|---|---|
| Origin | Who started it, for what business reason, on what matter | Purpose. The log holds the request, not the reason for it. |
| Authority | The named human who accepted the aggregate risk, and the date that acceptance lapses | A person. The log holds the identity that ran, not the identity that allowed. |
| Delegation | Agent to agent, scope by scope, timestamped | Scope. The log holds the handoff, not the permission behind it. |
| Effect boundary | What may be read, what may be changed, what may leave without review | The boundary. The log holds what was reached, not what was allowed to be reached. |

*Fifth element, and the one most often skipped: the trigger list. Which changes reopen this record before the chain runs again.*

# PART 3: THE AUTHORIZATION LAYER BENEATH THE MICROSOFT STACK

Four chapters on the layer that does not change when Microsoft's roadmap does. Chapter 10 names the missing floor beneath inventory, data, access, assurance, oversight, compliance, and audit. Chapter 11 designs the records that have to exist before an agent goes live. Chapters 12 and 13 take the platform's two strongest answers, identity and audit, and establish what each proves and what neither can.

---

# Chapter 10

# The Authorization Layer

On July 7, 2023, Commissioner Catherine Holmes delivered the report of the Royal Commission into the Robodebt Scheme: three volumes, 990 pages, 57 recommendations, and a sealed chapter recommending that specific individuals be referred for civil and criminal prosecution. The subject was an Australian government debt recovery program that had, for years, calculated welfare overpayments by averaging a citizen's annual tax office income across fortnights and raising a debt wherever the average said too much had been claimed. Fortnightly income is irregular for exactly the people such a program touches, the casual workers and students and people between jobs, and the averaging method could not see irregularity. The average said what averages say. The letters went out anyway, and the burden of proving the debt wrong rested on the person who opened the envelope.

The commission's findings run in a direction that should hold the attention of anyone who operates automated decision systems for a living, because the failure it documented was not primarily technical. The scheme was, in the report's words, "devised without regard to the social security law." The method itself, averaging as a basis for raising debts, was found "essentially unfair." One department secretary, the commission found, "did nothing of substance" when exposed to information that brought the scheme's illegality to light. Cabinet was misled. Sixteen current and former public servants were later referred for code of conduct investigation (Australian Public Service Commission, Robodebt Centralised Code of Conduct Inquiry, Commissioner's statement and Taskforce report, September 13, 2024), and the related class action had already settled at 1.8 billion Australian dollars (Royal Commission into the Robodebt Scheme, final report and media release, July 7, 2023). The report's own overview reaches for language no auditor would draft: "Robodebt was a crude and cruel mechanism, neither fair nor legal, and it made many people feel like criminals."

Hold the structure of those findings up to the light, because the structure is what this chapter is about. The operational machinery was mature. The program was a named government initiative with staffing, data flowing from the tax office through formal channels, a compliance workflow, a recoveries pipeline, and a public communications operation. It ran for years. Its outputs were issued, reviewed, appealed, and reported on. What it did not have, at any point in its life, was a validly made founding decision. The lawfulness of the method was never established before the machine was built around it, and no record of that establishment exists because the establishment never happened. Everything downstream, staffed by people doing their assigned jobs, was a competent implementation of a decision that was never validly made.

A royal commission is what an examination looks like when the examiner has subpoena power and the harm is national. Your version is smaller. It is also quieter, closer, and quite possibly running in your tenant right now: an agent whose monitoring is green, whose access is scoped, whose logs are complete, and whose founding decision, the one in which somebody with authority determined what it exists to do and put their own name against the consequences, is nowhere. Not lost. Never made. Everyone assumed it had been, which is a sentence this book has needed before and will need again.

## Six layers, all green

Be fair to the discipline first, because the discipline is real. Enterprise AI governance, as practiced and as audited, is a stack of operational layers, and every layer answers a genuine question. An inventory answers what systems exist. Data governance answers what they are trained and grounded on, and under what lineage and quality controls. Access control answers what they can reach and touch. Model assurance answers whether they behave as intended, within tolerances somebody can test. Human oversight answers which actions require a person before they take effect. Compliance and audit answer whether all of it can be evidenced against the regulations that apply. None of these is a bureaucratic invention. Each layer exists because its absence has produced documented harm, and an organization running all six is doing serious work.

Now run the Robodebt program through that stack and notice how little of it would have objected. The systems were known; this was a named initiative, not shadow IT. The data had provenance; it arrived from the tax office under formal arrangements. Access ran inside government systems under government authority. The outputs were reviewed and appealable. Records were produced at industrial scale. An assessor could have walked the layers, reviewed the data-sharing agreements and release records and audit trails a program like this generates, and issued a clean report about a program that was never legal to run, because none of the six layers was built to make the founding decision, and in most enterprises none is explicitly charged with checking that anyone did.

That is the geometry to sit with. The operational layers are horizontal; each governs an aspect of a system in motion. The question the commission spent 990 pages answering is vertical. It runs beneath all of them, down to the decision the entire stack was built on top of, and an organization can be excellent at every horizontal layer while nothing is at the bottom, because looking at the bottom is not any layer's job.

## The decision every layer stands on

Look at what each layer takes for granted. Assurance tests a system against its intended behavior, which presupposes that the intent was set down by someone entitled to set it. Oversight routes certain actions to a human, which presupposes that somebody decided which actions qualify and had the standing to decide. Audit checks conduct against permissions, which presupposes a permission that exists in checkable form. Every layer in the stack verifies something.

The thing at the bottom, the decision that this agent should operate, for this purpose, within these limits, on this named person's authority, is the one element of the architecture that no layer verifies. It is treated as a given. In most enterprises it is given by nobody.

Ask where that decision would live and the search is briefer than it should be. The closest artifact most organizations can produce is the procurement approval, and Chapter 3 already established what that document answers: who pays, not who decided. Past procurement, the trail runs through a project charter that authorized spending a budget, a change ticket that authorized a deployment window, and a security review that authorized a connection pattern. Each is an authorization of something adjacent. None is an authorization of the thing itself. Access was granted. Authorization was assumed.

The people-governance version of this gap would not survive a single quarter, which is what makes it useful to look at. Picture an employee three years into the job. Payroll runs. Performance reviews happen on schedule. The badge works, the laptop is patched, the manager-of-record field is populated. Then a dispute arises, employment counsel opens the personnel file, and there is no offer letter in it. Not a misplaced offer letter. No evidence that an offer was ever extended by anyone authorized to extend one, describing what the job is and on what terms. Every system that has hummed along for three years turns out to have been assuming a hiring decision that cannot be produced, and payroll running smoothly is not the same thing as anyone having hired him. Your agents are three years into the job.

## A crosswalk, constructed

What follows is a constructed scenario, in the same evidentiary spirit as the earlier ones: built to match documented regulatory patterns rather than drawn from any specific examination, and assembled from parts your organization already owns.

A European banking subsidiary is preparing for the EU AI Act's high-risk obligations, which, after the Digital Omnibus amendments the EU institutions finalized in June 2026, apply to standalone high-risk systems from December 2, 2027 (Regulation (EU) 2024/1689, as amended; Council final approval of the Digital Omnibus, June 29, 2026, verified July 11, 2026). The governance lead assembling the readiness file starts from the most complete list she has, the Agent 365 registry export: every agent the platform can see, each row carrying at least an identity, an owner, and a status. For each row that touches credit, employment, or anything else the regulation treats as high-risk, her file needs what the regulation, starting with Article 9's required risk management system, and her supervisors expect a governed system to have. A stated purpose. A risk assessment proportionate to that purpose. An accountable owner whose accountability was accepted somewhere, rather than inferred from a directory field.

The registry hands her the third column of a table whose first two columns are empty. The owner field is populated for most rows; the platform has been diligent about that. The stated purpose exists, where it exists, in a kickoff deck, an email thread, or the working memory of a product manager. The risk assessment exists for the four agents that passed through the model risk process, because they looked like models when they arrived. She checks the model inventory: four entries. She checks the automated decision-making inventory the bank built years ago for its rules engines: two more, both deterministic systems that predate the agents. The remaining rows on the export, which is most of them, live in no inventory that carries a use-case record, because they arrived as configurations, and nothing about a configuration announces itself to the processes that maintain those lists.

Her counterparts in the U.S. operation are not better off, only differently placed. SR 26-2, the interagency model risk guidance that superseded SR 11-7 in April 2026, excludes generative and agentic AI from model risk scope and directs institutions to cover the gap through risk management and governance practices of their own (Federal Reserve, OCC, FDIC, April 17, 2026). The one mature discipline that knows how to keep decision records about automated systems has stated, in writing, that these systems are outside its remit. So the regulation on one side of the Atlantic will ask for the record on a published date, and the supervisory guidance on the other side has already assigned the record to the institution. Neither will accept the registry export as a substitute, because the export is a list of what is running, and the question is what was decided. And when the gap surfaces in her bank, it will surface the way gaps surface in regulated institutions: as a written finding, agents operating without documented authorization of purpose, limits, or accountable owner, with a remediation deadline attached and the reconstruction done under it.

## A note on runtime enforcement

A newer class of tooling deserves a fair hearing here, because it will occur to every architect reading this chapter as the modern answer. At Build 2026, Microsoft released the Agent Control Specification as open source, an open specification within the Agent Governance Toolkit that enforces deterministic policy checks at five checkpoints in an agent's lifecycle: at input, at the model call, at state transitions, at tool execution, and at output (Microsoft Foundry Blog, June 2, 2026). Policy is expressed as portable, versionable files; a check can allow an action, block it, redact content, or route it to a human for approval (Agent Control Specification documentation, microsoft.github.io/agent-governance-toolkit, verified August 13, 2026). This is a genuine advance. It moves control from probabilistic instruction, telling a model what not to do and hoping, to structural enforcement at defined points, and it is built to travel across frameworks.

It also assumes exactly what every other layer in this chapter assumes. An execution boundary is an authorization decision that somebody wrote down in enforceable form. The deciding has to happen before the writing, and the specification, correctly, has no opinion about who does the deciding or where their decision is recorded. Adopt it without doing that underlying work and the machinery will still run: checks will fire at all five checkpoints, verdicts will be logged, and each one will enforce a policy nobody approved. Enforcement is downstream of a decision. It cannot substitute for one, and its logs, however complete, are evidence of enforcement, not evidence of deciding.

## The missing floor

The pattern has earned its name now, because you have watched it three times: in a royal commission's findings, in a readiness file with two empty columns, and in a runtime standard that enforces what somebody upstream was supposed to decide. Call it the Authorization Layer: the layer of decision and record beneath the operational stack, where someone with authority determines that this system should operate, defines what it is for and what it must not do, and accepts the consequences by name. The operational layers tell you the system is behaving. The authorization layer tells you it was ever allowed to.

The obligations beneath this layer are already in force. The layer itself is a design choice. Oversight, accountability, documentation, risk acceptance, and traceability are part of the job, and the problem is not that you need another duty. It is that each of those duties assumes a decision, and the record is where the decision becomes something you can hand to someone.

Naming the layer demotes nothing above it. Inventory, data governance, access control, assurance, oversight, and audit remain first-order obligations, and nothing in this chapter substitutes for any of them. The claim is narrower and harder. All six assume the same prior decision. All six are built to govern a system that decision permits. And when the decision is missing, all six operate anyway, at full quality, indefinitely, the way Robodebt's machinery did, until something outside the stack forces the vertical question. The commission's three volumes are what it costs to establish, after the fact and under oath, that the floor was never there.

The corporate version of that reckoning will not be a royal commission. It will be a request list arriving on a schedule you do not control, and a compliance team assembling a response folder, and the layers you have invested in will answer most of the items impressively. The item they cannot answer is the first one: who decided, and where is it written. That is not a tooling gap, and the platform cannot close it, because the platform was never the one deciding. Every control you run assumes an approval you never wrote. Your tenant's monitoring is green tonight, the boundaries are enforcing, and the floor beneath both is whatever you have been assuming it is.

---

**Six layers green, and the question none of them answers**

| The layer | What it proves | What it does not prove |
|---|---|---|
| Network | The traffic was permitted | That the traffic should have been requested |
| Identity | The actor was authenticated | That the actor was authorized for this |
| Access | The permission existed | That anyone decided it should |
| Data | The classification was enforced | That this agent should reach this class |
| Application | The action succeeded | That the action was sanctioned |
| Audit | The event was recorded | That a human ever approved the event |

*Every layer can report green while the deployment as a whole is unauthorized. The layers verify enforcement. Nothing beneath them holds the decision that enforcement is enforcing.*

# Chapter 11

# Intent Architecture for Microsoft Deployments

On November 2, 2021, Zillow filed an 8-K with the SEC. The exhibit was the quarter's shareholder letter, and the letter announced that Zillow Offers, the company's algorithmic home-buying operation, was being wound down. The operation had worked like this: forecasting models predicted what a home would resell for three to six months out, the company bought at prices those forecasts supported, and for a while the machine bought thousands of homes. In the third quarter the forecasts and the market parted ways, and Zillow took an inventory write-down of approximately 304 million dollars for buying homes above their resale estimates, disclosed another 240 to 265 million dollars of expected losses on homes it was still contractually obligated to purchase, and announced a workforce reduction of roughly 25 percent (Zillow Group Q3 2021 shareholder letter, 8-K exhibit, November 2, 2021).

Read the letter itself, because one sentence in it is doing work that deserves attention. Explaining the original decision, it says the company's aim in launching the program had been "to become a market maker, not a market risk taker," and it goes on to note that the company had publicly set unit-economic guardrails of plus or minus 200 basis points around breakeven. That is a purpose statement. It names what the system existed to do, states the risk posture it was authorized to hold, and even supplies a tolerance band an auditor could test against. It is plain enough for a board member and precise enough for an examiner. The clearest sentence ever written about what the system was for was written to explain why it was being shut down.

Be fair to Zillow, because the company was not ungoverned. It was a public company with a board, audited financials, and risk targets it had stated out loud to investors, which is more than most internal AI deployments can claim. The instructive fact is not that intent never existed. Executives plainly had it, and said so on earnings calls. The instructive fact is where the intent lived and what it could do from there. During operation it lived in strategy narratives and quarterly commentary, places built to persuade, while the system's actual boundaries lived in code and pricing parameters, places built to execute. If a document sat between them, one with authority over the system, stating its purpose, its limits, and what had to happen when performance left the stated band, the public record does not show it. The letter does not read like the product of one. When the unit economics swung far outside plus or minus 200 basis points, the response was not a review triggered by a record. It was a corporate decision made at write-down scale, explained afterward in a letter addressed to shareholders, because shareholders were the only constituency to whom the intent had ever been formally stated.

The version of this in your organization is smaller and has no press coverage. An agent is running in your tenant whose purpose exists in a kickoff deck on a SharePoint site, whose boundaries exist in an instructions field, and whose tolerance for going wrong exists in nobody's writing at all. If the question comes, and this book has spent ten chapters on the schedule by which the question comes, the document your organization produces will be written the way Zillow's was: after the fact, under pressure, addressed to whoever is asking, and accurate mainly about how it ended.

## Three decisions, in order

Take an agent your organization could build this quarter, described here as a hypothetical so its parts can be inspected. The servicing team at a mid-sized lender builds a payment-reminder agent in Copilot Studio. It reads the loan servicing system, drafts reminder emails to past-due accounts, offers a link to the payment portal, and hands anything complicated to a human collector. Useful, plausible, and the kind of thing a capable business user assembles in two weeks. Now watch what deciding, as opposed to configuring, would actually involve, because it comes in three layers and the order is not optional.

The first decision is about context, and it happens before anyone writes a word about purpose. Collection communications are among the most regulated messages a company can send: in the United States, Regulation F governs the content, frequency, and timing of covered collectors' communications (12 CFR Part 1006), and a bankruptcy flag or a cease-communication request converts a routine reminder into legal exposure. The affected people are, by definition, customers in financial distress, which is the stakeholder group regulators care most about. And the agent's reach is wider than its inbox: it reads the servicing system, sends through the corporate email infrastructure, and can open work items in the collections queue, which means three systems and their owners are inside its blast radius. None of this is about the agent. All of it determines what the agent can permissibly be for. An organization that skips this step is not saving time. It is discovering its regulatory environment later, through the environment's enforcement arm.

The second decision is the purpose itself, and the discipline is to write it so someone outside the building could evaluate it. One sentence about what problem the agent solves, in language a compliance officer can test conduct against. A scope stated as actions and data, not as model capabilities: it drafts reminders for accounts between five and sixty days past due, it reads these fields, it sends through this mailbox. And then the part that separates an authorization from a description: what it must not do. Never negotiate a settlement or a payment plan. Never contact an account carrying a bankruptcy or dispute flag. Never characterize what happens if the customer fails to pay. These prohibitions do not fall out of the configuration; each one is a decision a person makes because they can picture the harm, and the harms are not exotic. The reminder that lands on a bankruptcy-flagged account is a regulatory finding with a docket number waiting to happen, and the helpfully drafted sentence that reads like a promise of forbearance is a commitment the lender never made and now has to argue about. A prohibitions field left blank does not mean the organization prohibits nothing. It means nobody asked.

The third decision is about who answers, and it is the one organizations skip. A named person, call the role the Consequence Owner, accepts in writing that this agent's behavior is theirs to answer for, before it goes live rather than in the incident channel afterward. A review date goes on a calendar, and a short list of events forces the review early: the agent's data access changes, the regulations change, the owner changes, or an incident occurs. And someone writes the escalation path, which has a simple test. Ask the owner how the agent gets stopped and who gets called, and if the honest answer is the builder's phone number, the organization has a dependency, not a governance structure.

The order carries the logic. Context bounds what the intent may be. Intent gives governance something concrete to own and review. Run it backward, deploy first and reconstruct meaning later, and you get what most tenants contain today: configurations whose purpose is a matter of institutional memory, in organizations where memory has a two-year replacement cycle.

There is a plain-language name for what the agent in this state is missing. Organizations do not hire this way. A new employee arrives to a role somebody defined: what the job is, what it covers, what it does not cover, who it reports to. Strip that away and the failure is not immediate, because the person still shows up and does things. The failure arrives a year and a half later, in a performance conversation where the manager and the employee discover they never agreed on what the job was, and everything after that discovery is improvisation with stakes. The agent in your tenant has an identity, a license, connectors, and an owner field. It has everything the new hire gets except the job description, and it will never volunteer for the performance conversation.

## Where the layers land in the tenant

The Microsoft stack gives these decisions more surfaces than most organizations use, and precision about what each surface holds is worth the trouble, because the fragments are real and the record is not.

Start with the accountability fragment, which is the strongest. Microsoft Entra Agent ID gives every agent a directory identity carrying distinct owner and sponsor roles, and Microsoft's schema defines the sponsor as the human accountable for the agent's purpose and its lifecycle decisions (Microsoft Learn, verified July 4, 2026). That is the Consequence Owner's name, landed in a field, and the field placement differs by platform in a way earlier chapters have established: Copilot Studio writes the creator into it at the moment of creation, Microsoft Foundry leaves it assignable afterward. Either way the tenant can hold the name. What the tenant cannot hold is the acceptance. A sponsor field answers who is recorded. The third decision above is about who agreed, in a form that survives the person saying they never did, and a directory that can reassign the field automatically can keep it populated without anyone agreeing to anything.

The intent fragments are weaker, and looking at where they live explains why. A Copilot Studio agent carries a description, which is written for the people who will use the agent, and instructions, which are written for the model. Read that sentence again, because it locates the problem exactly. In many tenants the instructions field contains the only complete statement of what an agent should and should not do that exists anywhere, and its intended reader is the agent. Instructions are steering, tuned and retuned to shape behavior, edited by whoever maintains the agent, versioned nowhere the business can see. An authorization is a commitment, written for an examiner, signed by someone with authority, stable until deliberately revisited. The same words could not do both jobs even if the words were perfect, because the two documents answer to different audiences and change under different rules.

The context layer has the thinnest platform surface of all, and honestly so. The connectors tab enumerates what systems the agent can reach, which is capability, and knowledge-source lists enumerate what it can read, which is scope of a kind. But no field in the maker portal asks which regulations govern this use case, who is affected when it goes wrong, or which downstream owners have accepted the dependency, because those are not properties of the software. Chapter 3 established the category and it holds here without re-argument: the platform documents the deployment. The environment the deployment answers to is the organization's to map, and the mapping either exists as a pre-deployment artifact or gets performed for the first time by an examiner, on the examiner's schedule.

So the tenant, surveyed honestly, holds an identity, a sponsor's name, a capability list, and a set of instructions addressed to the model. Every layer has left a fragment, and the fragments are genuinely useful. What no surface holds is the decision in a form an examination could accept: examinable, durable, signed by someone with the authority to sign it. This is not a product defect to be fixed in a release. A decision about what an agent is for, made by people with authority to make it, recorded so that strangers can verify it later, is not the kind of thing that ships in a SKU.

## The standards question, asked federally

External confirmation that this is the live question arrived in February 2026, from an institution with no product to sell. NIST's National Cybersecurity Center of Excellence published a draft concept paper, "Accelerating the Adoption of Software and AI Agent Identity and Authorization," proposing a project to demonstrate how existing identity standards, OAuth and OpenID Connect among them, apply to enterprise AI agents, and opened it for public comment through April 2 (NCCoE, February 5, 2026). The paper's authorization section is a list of questions, and three of them reward a careful read: how can an agent prove its authority to perform a specific action, how might an agent convey the intent of its actions, and how can agent actions be logged and bound back to a human authorization in a form that supports non-repudiation.

Notice what kind of questions those are. Every one concerns conveyance: how authority, intent, and authorization travel with an action and get verified at the far end. The standards under consideration are transport engineering, tokens and assertions and delegation chains, and the paper takes no position on what the intent should say or who should have decided it, which is correct. That is not a standards body's decision to make. The federal machinery now being designed will carry organizational intent from wherever it is recorded to wherever it is checked. It will carry whatever exists. For most deployed agents, what exists is the instructions field.

## Four hundred agents

The objection arrives on cue whenever this design work is proposed, and it deserves a straight answer because it is half right. We cannot do this for four hundred agents. Correct: nobody can, at uniform depth, and nobody is being asked to. Documentation depth scales with what the agent can do wrong.

An internal agent that searches documents and summarizes them for the person who asked, touching nothing sensitive and writing nowhere, needs a lightweight record: purpose in a sentence, an owner, review triggers, with the context work done once for the whole class of agents like it. An agent that crosses departments, reads regulated data, or drafts things humans then act on needs the full treatment this chapter has walked: its own context, a purpose statement with explicit prohibitions, a named owner, a calendar. And an agent that communicates externally, moves money, or writes to systems of record that regulators treat as authoritative needs all of that plus sign-off before go-live and accountability that reaches board visibility, because its failures do. One caution belongs in writing wherever the tiers are adopted: the tiering governs internal effort, not legal exposure, and an agent your triage calls medium can still be high-risk in a regulator's classification. The tier decides how much you write down. It does not decide what you are liable for.

Framed this way, the four-hundred-agents objection concedes the point. Sorting four hundred agents into three tiers requires knowing what each one is for and what it can reach. That is to say, the objection cannot even be operationalized without doing the first layer of the work it objects to. The triage is the beginning of the record.

## The design layer

The work this chapter has been walking has a name. Intent Architecture is the organizational design layer that defines what an agent is authorized to do before it does anything, and the Intent Architecture Stack is its operating form, three layers in fixed order. Context: the regulatory obligations, affected stakeholders, and system integrations that determine what the intent can permissibly be. Intent: the purpose in plain language, the authorized scope, the explicit prohibitions, the expected outputs and their human-review triggers. Governance: the named Consequence Owner, the review cadence with its event triggers, the escalation path that works without the builder. The word architecture is doing deliberate work in the name. Architecture is what gets decided before anything is built, and an organization deciding after deployment what an agent should have been authorized to do is not doing architecture. It is doing forensics on its own intentions.

The stack is platform-independent by design, and this chapter has kept its Microsoft application honest: the tenant supplies fields for fragments of all three layers and an examinable home for none of them. That is the correct division of labor. It is uncomfortable only for organizations that assumed the platform's half was the whole. And when the record does not exist, the distance between what the organization meant and what production does, the Intent

Gap, opens on the first day and belongs to no one. A gap can only be measured from a fixed point and nobody fixed one.

Which returns everything to the question of what your organization could produce today. The connectors are enumerated. The permissions are scoped. The identity is in the directory with a name in the sponsor field. Reach, in other words, is documented to a standard any examiner would admire, because reach is what the platform records without being asked. We wrote down what the agent can reach. Nobody wrote down what it was for. And of the two documents, the one that does not exist is the one that gets harder to write every day the agent runs, because a purpose written after the question arrives is not an authorization. Zillow already showed you what it is. It is an explanation.

---

### Three layers, three records

| Layer | The record it produces | The question it answers | What its absence looks like in an examination |
|---|---|---|---|
| **Context** | The environment record | What can this agent reach, and under whose permissions? | "We can tell you what it accessed. We cannot tell you what it was entitled to access." |
| **Intent** | The purpose record | What was this agent approved to accomplish, and for whom? | "It was approved. We are locating the description of what was approved." |
| **Governance** | The accountability record | Who signed, when, and on what expiry? | "The team that built it has moved on." |

*A deployment can be strong at one layer and silent at the other two. The examination tests the weakest.*

## Chapter 12

# Microsoft Entra Agent ID and What Identity Doesn't Solve

In the Microsoft Entra admin center, under Entra ID, then Agents, then Agent identities, your tenant keeps a page for every agent it knows about. Pick one and read it the way an examiner would, top to bottom, because for many tenants this page is the most complete document the organization holds about the agent, and the reading takes about ninety seconds.

The display name is at the top, human-friendly and changeable. Below it sits the object ID, a string of hexadecimal that uniquely identifies this agent in your tenant and appears wherever the agent acts. Status: enabled. Created On: a date, probably one nobody in the room remembers. A Blueprint App ID links the agent back to the template it was created from, the agent identity blueprint, which defines what kind of agent this is and holds the security posture every agent of its kind inherits. There is a panel for owners and sponsors, and both fields are populated: an owner, who administers the thing, and a sponsor, a human name, held out by the schema as the person who answers for why the agent exists and how long it should keep existing. There is a list of granted permissions, each one enumerable, each one scoped. The sign-in logs are one click away, and they are good logs: every token this agent has acquired, against which resource, with what outcome, filterable down to the agent's specific identity type.

One detail rewards a second look. The credentials section is not what a security reviewer braced for, because the agent identity holds no credentials of its own. It acquires tokens through its blueprint, which is where the credentials actually live, which means there is no per-agent secret to leak, rotate, or forget in a config file (Microsoft Learn, agent identity anatomy, verified July 11, 2026).

Now notice what you have read. Every field on this page describes the agent. Its name, its lineage, its permissions, its activity, its accountable human. Not one field describes a decision. Nothing on the page records that anyone with authority determined this agent should exist, examined what it would be permitted to do, weighed what it must never do, and accepted the consequences in writing. The page is an identity. You went looking for an authorization, and the tenant handed you a passport.

This chapter is the fairest hearing Microsoft gets in Part 3, because the identity layer deserves one. What Microsoft Entra Agent ID does, it does well, and an organization that skips it is making its problem worse. The argument here is narrower and harder to fix: identity work and authorization work are different kinds of work, the directory was built for one of them, and the better the directory gets, the easier it becomes to mistake it for the other.

## What the directory proves

Start with what the page can honestly testify to, because it is more than skeptics assume.

The directory now treats agents as a distinct population. Microsoft Entra Agent ID models them through four object types: the agent identity blueprint, the blueprint's principal, the agent identity itself, and, where an agent genuinely needs to act as a user, an agent's user account bound one-to-one to its agent identity (Microsoft Learn, Entra Agent ID documentation, verified July 11, 2026). This matters for a plain reason. An agent that exists in the directory as an agent, rather than hiding inside the undifferentiated mass of service principals, can be counted, filtered, and questioned as an agent. The sign-in logs carry an agent-specific event type, the audit logs carry an agentType property on the actor of an event, and the admin center offers a filter whose two options summarize a decade of identity architecture arriving somewhere new: Is Agent, yes or no (Microsoft Learn, Entra Agent ID logs, verified July 11, 2026). The labels and filter strings will have moved by the time you read this, because admin center strings always move. The pattern is the durable part: the agent, queryable as itself.

The credential model is genuinely disciplined. Credentials attach to the blueprint, not to each running instance, and Microsoft's guidance steers production deployments toward managed identities and federated credentials rather than secrets (Microsoft Learn, Agent ID best practices, verified July 11, 2026).

Conditional Access policies can be applied at the blueprint level, where every current and future instance inherits them. And disabling a blueprint immediately blocks every agent identity created from it, which gives a security team something it rarely has in an incident: one switch that stops a whole class of actor at the identity layer.

Attribution, the thing audit trails live or die on, is served properly. When an agent acts, the log shows the agent, not a shared service account, not a borrowed human login. The examiner who asks what this agent did on the night of the fourteenth can be answered from the directory's own records, down to the token.

And the schema carries an accountability field. The sponsor is the person or group the tenant records as answerable for the agent: for deciding when it is no longer needed, for approving extensions when its access expires, for authorizing its suspension during an incident. The sponsor is deliberately distinct from the owner, who handles technical administration (Microsoft Learn, owners and sponsors for agent identities, verified July 11, 2026). Sponsorship even plugs into identity governance, so that lifecycle workflows can react when a sponsor leaves the company, a machinery whose failure mode Chapter 2 already examined at machine speed. This is a better identity story than most organizations can tell about their contractors.

All of it is real. All of it is necessary. An organization without this layer cannot even locate its accountability gap, because it cannot reliably say which actor did what. The trouble begins when the organization concludes that a directory this good must be answering the authorization question too, because the directory is not, and cannot, and the reason is not a missing feature. The misreading is routine in practice: a populated sponsor field and a clean permission list get presented, in access reviews and to auditors, as though they were the approval itself.

## The proof boundary

Identity systems answer one question: is this actor who it claims to be. Everything on the agent's page serves that question. The object ID makes the agent unambiguous, the blueprint makes its provenance legible, the credentials make its tokens trustworthy, the logs make its actions attributable. This is authentication and its bookkeeping, and when it works, you know with cryptographic confidence which agent did the thing.

Authorization is not a stronger version of that question. It is a different question aimed at a different object. An authorization is a claim about a decision: that a person with the authority to commit the organization decided this agent should exist, defined what it is for, bounded what it may and must not do, and accepted answerability for the result. The evidence for a claim like that cannot be generated by the actor's own infrastructure, however well instrumented, because the thing being proved did not happen inside the infrastructure. It happened, if it happened, in the organization: in a meeting, a review, a signature. The directory can carry a reference to such a decision. It cannot constitute one, any more than a passport constitutes permission to work in the country that stamps it. The passport proves who you are, to a standard border agents worldwide accept. The visa is a different document, issued by a different authority, answering a different question: what you were permitted to do here. Microsoft Entra Agent ID issues passports, excellent ones. The visa office is not in the product, because the visa office is your organization.

The sponsor field is where this boundary gets tested, so look at it closely. As the schema now stands, the name is close to guaranteed: an agent identity blueprint cannot be created without a sponsor, Microsoft's guidance calls for at least one sponsor on every agent identity as well, and in the guided setup flows the sponsor defaults to whoever is signed in when the wizard asks (Microsoft Learn, blueprint creation and Zero Trust guidance for agent identities, verified July 11, 2026). A mandatory field guarantees the presence of a name. It cannot guarantee that the name's owner decided anything, or knows, or agreed, which is the acceptance problem Chapter 5 traced from the named person's side. The failure mode assembles itself from defaults: a platform team publishes a standard blueprint, the sponsor field takes the name of the engineer who happened to build it, the engineer holds no authority to commit the organization to anything, and the field goes on certifying accountability through two reorganizations. The schema also permits a dynamic membership group as sponsor, meaning the accountable party can be whoever currently matches a rule, re-evaluated on the directory's own schedule. Accountability as a query result is a genuinely new contribution to the field. It means an organization can now answer the question of who is accountable by running a query that no human being has ever read, let alone agreed to.

The fault here is not the field's. A directory attribute is written for the directory's own workflows, the same split Chapter 11 located between words written to steer a system and words written to answer an examiner. The sponsor field exists so that lifecycle automation has a human to route to and an incident commander has a human to call. Those are good reasons for a field. They are not evidence of a decision, and even the standards work now underway on agent identity keeps this line: the NIST concept paper on agent identity and authorization treats how an agent might prove its authority as an open question, and takes no position on where the authority is supposed to come from. Transport is being engineered. Cargo remains the customer's problem.

## When the question reaches a person

If the distinction feels academic, the case law says otherwise, and the case worth sitting with involves no AI at all. On October 5, 2022, a federal jury in the Northern District of California convicted Joseph Sullivan, formerly Uber's chief security officer, on two counts: obstruction of an FTC proceeding, and misprision of a felony. The conduct underneath the charges was concealment. Attackers had gotten hold of records on 57 million Uber riders and drivers in 2016, and rather than disclose it, the company paid the intruders 100,000 dollars, moved the money through its bug bounty program, and wrapped the arrangement in nondisclosure agreements. Sullivan's sentence, handed down in May 2023, was three years of probation and a 50,000-dollar fine (Department of Justice, N.D. Cal., press releases, October 5, 2022 and May 4, 2023).

Be precise about what convicted him, because the precision is the lesson. Sullivan was not convicted for the breach itself, and not for how the intruders got in. He was convicted for the account his organization gave of the event afterward, the concealment, the gap between what happened and what was disclosed. The relevance to this chapter is structural. When the questions about what had happened inside Uber's systems finally came, they were not addressed to the infrastructure. They were addressed to a named human, under oath, in a courtroom, and what mattered was whether the organization's account of its own systems could survive scrutiny. Your agents are privileged non-human actors accumulating exactly that kind of question, and when it arrives, it will not land on the blueprint or the sign-in logs either. The directory will attribute their actions flawlessly. The account of why they were permitted to act, the part a named person may one day have to stand behind personally, is the part no log produces.

## The population the passport office never met

One more limit belongs in the record, and it is about coverage rather than category. The directory's count of agents begins at the directory's own definition of one. Copilot Studio agents built before the July 2026 identity cutover still authenticate through legacy app registrations, which the directory files under applications, not agents. The Power Automate flow fleet, performing standing delegated work under human credentials, sits outside most agent-inventory definitions entirely. Chapter 8's registry has begun converting some of this darkness into a dashboard, tile by tile, but the principle survives the tooling: an identity system can only prove things about the actors it was introduced to. The agents your organization most needs to ask hard questions about have a way of predating the paperwork.

## Necessary, and insufficient, and why the order matters

Here is the chapter's claim, stated plainly. An identity system executes decisions. Provisioning an agent identity executes a decision that the agent should exist. Granting a permission executes a decision about scope. A Conditional Access policy executes a decision about constraint. Disabling a blueprint executes a decision to stop. Every operation the directory performs is downstream of a decision made somewhere else, by someone, or by no one. When the decisions exist, the directory is the best execution layer for them that Microsoft has ever shipped, and this book's later chapters on the authorization record assume you are using it. When the decisions do not exist, the directory executes anyway. The agent gets an identity, a required sponsor, scoped permissions, and pristine logs, and the whole apparatus runs as designed, to the letter, on top of a decision nobody made.

That is why the examiner reading the agent's page in the admin center learns everything about the agent and nothing about the decision. The page was never lying. It is an execution record, maintained by an execution layer, and it is the wrong place to look for the thing that was supposed to come first. The directory can prove the agent is yours. It cannot prove you decided anything.

So take the ninety seconds. Open the admin center tonight, pull up one agent identity, and read the sponsor field. There is a name in it; the schema made sure of that. The question the schema cannot answer, and that this page will eventually be held up next to, is whether the person behind the name decided anything at all, and whether anything in your organization would show it if they had.

For most tenants the honest answer is that the field was populated the day the wizard demanded a value, and has been quietly certifying accountability ever since, to everyone who reads it except the person it names.

## Chapter 13

# Microsoft Purview as Governance Backbone (and Its Limits)

On June 15, 2023, a security operations center at the United States Department of State noticed something wrong in the access patterns of its mail systems. The next day, analysts watched alerts fire from a custom detection rule the department had built and named, internally, Big Yellow Taxi. The rule watched a single log: MailItemsAccessed, a record of which items in which Exchange Online mailboxes had been opened, by whom, through what application. Something with the wrong application identity was reading mail it had no business reading (Cyber Safety Review Board, Review of the Summer 2023 Microsoft Exchange Online Intrusion, report dated March 20, 2024, released April 2, 2024).

The something was a threat actor Microsoft tracks as Storm-0558, associated with the government of the People's

Republic of China. It had acquired, by means Microsoft has never been able to establish, a consumer signing key that Microsoft issued in 2016, and it used that key to forge authentication tokens. A flaw in token validation meant Exchange Online accepted tokens signed by the consumer key for enterprise mailboxes it should never have opened. With that combination, Storm-0558 read the cloud mailboxes of 22 organizations and 503 personal accounts; among the official accounts it read were those of the most senior U.S. officials managing the country's relationship with China. From the State Department alone it downloaded roughly 60,000 emails. It had been inside for at least six weeks before Big Yellow Taxi sang (CSRB report, April 2024).

Hold the two halves of that story next to each other. The forged key, the validation flaw, the six weeks of quiet reading: those belong to Microsoft, and the Cyber Safety Review Board's report assigns them to Microsoft in language boards rarely use, concluding that the intrusion "should never have happened." But the detection belongs to a customer. State found the intrusion because it could see the MailItemsAccessed log, and it could see that log because it had purchased a specific license, the government G5 tier, which included a product then called Microsoft Purview Audit (Premium). Victims without that tier did not have the log. The Board recorded what that meant in practice: Microsoft turned on enhanced logging for victims it identified, but organizations that lacked the premium license at the time of the intrusion could not see backward into it. The evidence of what had been done to them existed as a capability. They had not bought it.

Say it plainly, because the plain version is the chapter. In the summer of 2023, the ability to know whether a foreign intelligence service was reading your executives' mail was a SKU: a line item on a price list, present in some tenants and absent from others, and the difference between the victim who noticed and the victims who did not was, at bottom, a purchasing decision nobody had understood themselves to be making. The organizations that could not see the intrusion were not less attacked. They were less subscribed.

The pressure that followed was public and fast. On July 19, 2023, Microsoft announced, jointly with the Cybersecurity and Infrastructure Security Agency, that it would move MailItemsAccessed and more than thirty other log types into the standard audit tier at no additional cost, rolling out from September 2023, and would extend the standard tier's default log retention from 90 days to 180 (Microsoft Security Blog, July 19, 2023; CISA announcement, same date). CISA's director praised the change as a step toward security that does not arrive as an upsell. By January 2025, CISA had published a sixty-page playbook teaching organizations how to actually use the logs they now had (CISA, Microsoft Expanded Cloud Logs Implementation Playbook, January 2025). The specific gap that hid Storm-0558, that one log type at that one tier, is closed.

The category of gap is not, and it has just acquired a new population. Your agents are generating evidence right now, in Microsoft Purview, under retention defaults and licensing tiers and enablement toggles that somebody in your organization either decided or inherited. This chapter is about that evidence: what Purview genuinely captures about agents, which is a great deal;

what the captured record can and cannot say; what sits underneath it in the systems the agents actually change; and the question Storm-0558 forces on all of it, which is not whether the log is good. It is whether anyone in your organization ever decided what evidence you would be able to produce, or whether, like most of the 2023 victims, you are running on a default you have never read.

## What the tenant records

Purview's coverage of agent activity deserves to be stated generously, because it is the broadest evidence surface in the book so far and most organizations have not absorbed how much of it is already on.

When a user interacts with Microsoft 365 Copilot, or with an agent built in Copilot Studio, or with a custom application built on Microsoft Foundry, the interaction lands in the Purview unified audit log automatically, as part of Audit (Standard), with no configuration required beyond auditing being enabled for the tenant; the record is generated where the surface is licensed and in use. The record identifies who interacted, when, where, and which files, sites, and resources the system touched to generate its response, sensitivity labels included (Microsoft Learn, audit logs for Copilot and AI applications, and the Microsoft Purview service description, verified July 11, 2026). Chapter 3 opened on one of these rows and read it as an evidence exhibit. The exhibit is produced, today, across the major Microsoft agent surfaces, and coverage follows the product line as new surfaces ship.

The prompts and responses themselves are kept, and kept somewhere with legal machinery attached. For Microsoft 365 Copilot and Copilot Studio, that content is stored in a hidden folder of the interacting user's Exchange mailbox, which sounds like an implementation detail until you notice what it inherits: mailbox content is subject to retention policies, eDiscovery search, and litigation hold, so an agent conversation can be preserved, collected, and produced in a legal matter through the same tooling an organization already uses for mail. Microsoft Foundry sits in a different retention location, alongside the other enterprise AI apps, and its prompt and response content is captured only where an administrator has configured a collection policy to capture it (Microsoft Learn, retention for Copilot and AI apps, verified August 3, 2026). Two of those surfaces keep the conversation because keeping it is what they do. The third keeps it if somebody decided it should. Data Security Posture Management for AI sits on top, surfacing which AI applications are in use, retrieving interaction transcripts, and flagging risky prompts and sensitive-data flows for review (Microsoft Learn, Purview for Copilot Studio, verified July 11, 2026).

Coverage extends, conditionally, beyond Microsoft's own applications. Interactions with non-Microsoft AI applications can be logged too, under a pay-as-you-go billing model: the logs are not included in the enterprise subscription, are off until someone enables them, are billed by the volume of records ingested, and are retained for 180 days (Microsoft Learn, audit-copilot, verified August 13, 2026). Read that sentence again as a governance artifact rather than a feature description. The evidence trail for every agent your organization runs outside the Microsoft family exists behind a toggle that defaults to off and a meter that runs when it is on. Whether that toggle has been flipped in your tenant is a fact about your organization, not about Microsoft, and it is exactly the kind of fact the summer of 2023 was made of.

As of mid-2026, then, the honest inventory reads: automatic interaction capture for Microsoft agent surfaces, transcripts under eDiscovery and hold, a posture dashboard for AI use, and opt-in metered capture for everything else. The capability tiers and retention figures in this section move quickly and are stated as of July 11, 2026; the durable point survives any repricing. Purview will hold more evidence about your agents than your organization holds about most of its employees. What that evidence can prove is the next question.

## What the record executes

Chapter 3 established what the audit row contains and the category it cannot contain, and one clause carries it here: the row shows the action and the label, never the sanction. This section is about a subtler limit, one that lives in the controls themselves, because Purview is not only a recorder. It enforces. Sensitivity labels classify content; data loss prevention policies act on the classifications, blocking a share, restricting what labeled content an agent may process, warning a user, logging an event. It is tempting, and increasingly common, to present the label taxonomy and the DLP policy set to an auditor as the organization's agent authorization in enforceable form. Here is the scope we decided; here is the machine that holds it.

The presentation fails on its own evidence, in two directions.

First, a DLP policy expresses a decision only if the decision happened. The policy object in the tenant proves that a rule exists, who last modified it, and when it fired. It does not prove that anyone with authority over the business decided the rule's scope was the right scope for agents, because in most tenants the label taxonomy and the policy set were written years before agents arrived, for a different threat: people attaching spreadsheets to outbound mail. The agent inherited the policy the way it inherited the tenant. An examiner who asks who decided these boundaries were appropriate for autonomous retrieval and generation is not asking when the policy was created. Chapter 10 drew the general boundary between enforcement and deciding. What this surface adds is the specific failure of evidence: the policy's audit trail testifies to its own maintenance, not to its mandate.

Second, and less comfortably, the coverage of the enforcement is exactly the coverage of the labeling effort, and the gaps are silent. A DLP policy scoped to labeled content governs the content somebody got around to labeling. Everything unlisted and unlabeled rides the default, and the default is that nothing fires. On the evidence side this produces a trap worth naming: the absence of DLP events for an agent is routinely read as the agent behaving, when it is equally consistent with the agent operating almost entirely in content the labeling program never reached. Silence from the enforcement layer is not a clean bill. It is a map of where the map ends. In an examination, the unlabeled majority of the tenant does not appear as a finding about the agent. It appears as a finding about the organization, which is worse.

This is no argument against labels or DLP; an organization without them has less evidence and less control, not more. The argument is about what kind of exhibit they make. They are the executed half of a scope decision. Produced alone, they invite the question they cannot answer, which is where the decided half lives.

## The floor under the agents

Everything so far has been about interaction evidence: what the agent was asked, what it answered, what it read along the way. But agents are deployed to change things, not to converse, and the things they change live in systems of record. In a Microsoft estate, that floor is concrete and nameable: Dataverse tables under Copilot Studio agents and Power Platform flows, SharePoint libraries under Microsoft 365 Copilot, Exchange mailboxes under anything that reads or sends mail, Dynamics 365 records under agents working sales, service, and finance. When an examiner moves from what did the agent say to what did the agent do, the evidence question moves down a layer, and the quality of the answer depends on properties the substrate either has or lacks.

Walk the floor the way a reviewer would, asking five things of each system.

Does it hold durable, identifiable records, or loose content? A Dataverse row and a Dynamics case are records: they persist, they have identities, they can be pointed at. An email thread is content; a mailbox is a conversation that never signed anything. An agent can act on a thread. No examiner can reconstruct a business decision from one without a human narrating it.

Does it enforce legal state transitions, or accept any label at any time? A Dynamics case that moves from active to resolved under defined conditions is a state machine; the record itself knows which changes were lawful. A SharePoint document with a Status column anyone can edit is wearing a costume.

Is ownership a field with a name in it, or an inference? Dataverse and Dynamics carry owner columns on the row itself. A document library's answer is often whoever last touched it, which is not an answer an agent can act on and not one an examiner will accept.

Are the verbs formal or conversational? Create, assign, resolve, approve, and close have semantics a log can carry. Reply, forward, and comment do not; they are the verbs of content, and an agent operating in them leaves a trail of activity with no grammar of consequence.

And can the history be queried, or only viewed? Dataverse auditing produces change history an investigator can interrogate: filter it, pull it out of the system, hand it over as an exhibit. But the capability is a configuration, not a constant. Auditing is enabled per environment and per table, and a substrate whose auditing nobody turned on has this chapter's missing-evidence problem one layer down. A history that exists only as a screen someone can scroll is testimony that cannot be subpoenaed in bulk.

Score the Microsoft floor honestly and it comes out uneven in an instructive way. Dataverse, and Dynamics riding on it, hold up well on all five, which is one reason the platform steers serious agent work toward them. SharePoint is genuinely mixed: a governed list with enforced columns behaves like a record system, while the ordinary document library that hosts most of a company's actual work is content wearing a site's clothing. Exchange fails the walk almost entirely, and not for lack of instrumentation: mailbox auditing captures activity and litigation hold preserves content, but the walk asks about records, states, owners, and verbs. A mailbox has none of them. And Exchange is where an enormous share of agent activity lives, because it is where the humans live.

Now notice what even a perfect score buys. A substrate that passes all five questions can tell you, durably and queryably, what changed, when, and under which identity. Chapter 12 established what identity attribution proves and where it stops, and the same boundary arrives here intact one layer down. The row that changed cannot say whether the change was supposed to happen: whether a business condition sanctioned it, whether the write sat inside any scope a named human approved, whether a person was required in the loop and was there. The substrate's audit history is the platform's half of an answer. The sanction is the organization's half, and no property of Dataverse, at any license tier, will ever supply it. This two-tier walk, structural properties first and then the authorization the structure cannot express, is published in this book's framework library as the Agent Substrate Readiness Model; the version here is scoped to the Microsoft floor, and the multi-substrate version, for estates that also run Jira, Salesforce, ServiceNow, SAP, and Workday, lives in the library. What it surfaces is the production an examination will eventually demand: the change from the system, the sanction from you, joined.

## Who decided how long the evidence lives

One decision remains, and it is the one Storm-0558 should have permanently changed how you read: the lifespan of the evidence itself.

The current defaults are easy to state. Audit logs in the standard tier are retained for 180 days, a figure that has its own history, because it was 90 until Microsoft raised it in the wake of the 2023 intrusion, effective for logs generated on or after October 17, 2023 (Microsoft Learn, auditing solutions, verified July 11, 2026). The premium audit tier holds the core workloads, Entra ID, Exchange, SharePoint, and OneDrive, for one year by default. Everything else stays at 180 days unless a policy extends it, and ten-year retention is its own add-on license (Microsoft Learn, Purview service description and audit-log-retention-policies, verified July 12, 2026, re-verified August 2, 2026). Pay-as-you-go logs for non-Microsoft AI applications live 180 days. Agent prompts and responses in the mailbox follow whatever retention policy the organization has configured for Copilot experiences, if it has configured one.

Every regulated organization already knows what a decision about evidence lifespan looks like, because every regulated organization has a records-retention schedule: a document, owned by legal or compliance, that says what categories of record exist, how long each is kept, and on whose authority, reviewed on a cycle, signed. Nobody treats the retention of contracts or trade records as a storage feature that arrived with the filing cabinets. Retention is a policy someone signs, not a default someone inherits. Then the same organization deploys agents whose entire evidentiary existence, interaction logs, transcripts, substrate change history, runs on retention figures that appear in no schedule, were reviewed by no counsel, and are, in the standard tier, a number that Microsoft and a federal agency negotiated on the organization's behalf in the aftermath of somebody else's breach.

Set the number against the clocks that matter. Chapter 1's tribunal read a chatbot conversation more than a year after it happened. Regulatory examinations routinely reach back through multiple years of activity; internal investigations and litigation reach back further. Against those windows, 180 days is not a retention policy. It is a head start for the question you have not been asked yet. An organization that has never compared its audit retention to its examination exposure has made the comparison anyway, by default, and the default's answer is that the evidence will be gone.

So end where the chapter began, with the difference between State and everyone else in the summer of 2023. It was not budget; several victims could have afforded the license. It was not tooling; the log existed, one tier up. The difference was that somewhere in one organization, at some point before the attack, people decided what they needed to be able to see, bought it, staffed it, and wrote a detection rule with a joke in its name, so that when the day came the evidence was there and someone was reading it. Every element of that sentence is a decision, and each has an agent-shaped version sitting in your tenant tonight: the tier your audit runs at, the toggle for the agents Microsoft did not build, the retention policy on the transcripts, the auditing settings on the tables your agents write to, and the name of the person who owns those choices, if there is one. The platform has already made its version of each decision and shipped it to you as a default. The log's retention was a licensing decision. The examiner will read it as a governance one.

### The substrate's half, and the half it cannot hold

| The examination asks | The substrate answers | Why the answer stops there |
|---|---|---|
| What changed? | The row, the field, the value before and after | A change record describes an event, not a decision |
| When did it change? | The timestamp, durably and queryably | Timing establishes sequence, not sanction |
| Under which identity? | The agent identity that performed the write | Identity establishes the actor, not the permission |
| Did a business condition sanction it? | Nothing | No property of the substrate encodes the condition |
| Was the write inside an approved scope? | Nothing | The scope was never recorded here to begin with |
| Was a required human in the loop? | Nothing | Presence is not a field any license tier keeps |

*Three rows the platform fills, three it leaves blank, and an examination that asks for all six joined. The blank half is not a gap in the product. It is the half the organization was always going to have to write.*

# PART 4: THE OPERATING MODEL

Authorization is not a document an organization writes once, and this part is about running it. Chapter 14 reconciles what the tenant contains against what the organization approved. Chapter 15 keeps approvals current while agents change underneath them, and Chapter 16 converts monitoring signals into decisions somebody is obligated to make. Chapter 17 closes the part as its stress test: the newest vendor answer, and what it still cannot prove.

# Chapter 14

# Tenant Agent Reconciliation in Microsoft Environments

In December 2021, enterprise security teams around the world learned, more or less simultaneously, that they could not answer a basic question about their own environments: where does our software run?

The trigger was a flaw in Log4j, a free, open-source logging library maintained by a handful of volunteers under the Apache Software Foundation. Log4j did unglamorous work. It wrote log entries, the timestamped lines of text that applications produce about their own behavior, and it did that work so well and so cheaply that developers had been folding it into Java software for two decades. The flaw, disclosed publicly in December 2021 and scored at the maximum severity the vulnerability scoring system awards, allowed an attacker to run code on any machine that logged a line of text the attacker controlled. That would have been a bad month under any circumstances. It became a defining one because of where Log4j lived: inside commercial products, cloud platforms, industrial equipment, and custom applications, frequently as a dependency of a dependency, invisible even to the teams that had shipped it.

The response, not the flaw, is what this chapter is about. The Cyber Safety Review Board, the federal body created to study major cyber events the way transportation boards study crashes, took Log4j as its first case and published its review on July 11, 2022. Read the report today and the most consequential finding is not technical. It is clerical. There was no comprehensive list of where Log4j ran, the Board found, "or even a list of where it is integrated as a sub-system," and that absence, more than any property of the exploit, is what turned a patchable bug into a global emergency. Organizations could not fix what they could not find. One federal cabinet department reported spending 33,000 hours on its Log4j response (Cyber Safety Review Board, Review of the December 2021 Log4j Event, July 11, 2022). That is roughly sixteen work-years, spent answering a question that an accurate inventory would have answered in an afternoon. The Board concluded that Log4j had become an "endemic vulnerability," likely to persist in systems for years, perhaps a decade or longer, and its recommendations led not with better cryptography or smarter detection but with the humblest control in the catalog: know what you have. Asset inventories. Software bills of materials. Lists.

Sit with how ordinary the failure was. The component was not malicious. The organizations that lost those months were not careless; many of them ran mature security programs with real budgets. They had simply never been required to enumerate a class of thing that had been accumulating in their environments for twenty years, unit by unit, each arrival individually reasonable and no arrival recorded anywhere that could later be queried. Chapter 2 measured this enterprise instinct in an earlier wave: information technology departments estimated fifty-one cloud services in use while the network traffic showed 730. Now hold the pattern up against the class of thing accumulating in your Microsoft tenant right now. Agents arrive the way Log4j did, one reasonable decision at a time, folded into departments and workflows by people solving real problems with tools the organization gave them. The difference is that a logging library waits to be exploited. An agent acts.

## The count the platform ships

Give the platform its due before asking what remains, because the enumeration half of this problem has been productized with real seriousness. Chapter 8 walked the Agent 365 registry in full: a single admin center surface that lists the tenant's agents across the platforms its discovery and integrations reach, summarizes the fleet in counter tiles, and flags as risks the agents no one owns and the agents the documentation defines as operating outside the plane's protection, with the whole picture exportable on demand (Microsoft Learn, agent registry documentation, verified July 10, 2026). The tile names will drift as the product does; what the argument rests on is the functions, a count, a risk view, an export. What the Log4j responders spent work-years assembling by hand, an agent-shaped version now renders on a dashboard, continuously, for every tenant that turns it on. Chapter 8 also established what that visibility converts ignorance into, and one clause carries it here: a count on a screen is notice, dated and preserved.

So the running count, the number that took 33,000 hours to approximate for one software component, arrives nearly free. And a reconciliation needs two numbers. The second one is the count of agents your organization decided to operate: reviewed, scoped, and approved by someone with the authority to accept what the agent might do. No tile shows it. Not because the engineering is hard but because the number is not in the telemetry, or anywhere else a platform can reach. It exists if your organization wrote it down, approval by approval, and it does not exist otherwise. No agent joins the approved count by appearing on a screen; it joins when a person with authority signs something. The platform can inventory what runs in the tenant. Only the organization can inventory what it agreed to.

Every warehouse operator on earth already understands this structure. A distribution business keeps a ledger, the book record of what stock should be on the shelves, and once a year it counts the shelves, and the audit requirement is the reconciliation of the two, because no auditor accepts the ledger as the count and no auditor accepts the count as the ledger. The difference between them has a name, shrinkage, and a line in the financials. Now look at the agent estate through that lens and notice the inversion. The warehouse's hard problem was always the physical count; the ledger was the easy part, kept by default, because it never occurred to anyone to run a business without a book record of what they own. The agent estate has the opposite shape. The count is now automated and the ledger was never started. Enterprises have solved the half of the reconciliation that machines can do, which was never the half that was missing.

## One reconciliation, constructed

What follows is a constructed exercise, in the same spirit as this book's earlier scenarios: not drawn from any specific organization, and it requires nothing your organization does not already own.

A mid-sized insurer. In March, the audit committee asks the chief risk officer a one-line question, the kind that sounds polite in the minutes: how many AI agents does the company operate, and under what approvals? The CRO discovers that no honest answer exists and assigns the question to the head of operational risk, who convenes a small team and gives it a quarter, scoped honestly: the quarter buys the count and the catalog, not the governing of everything counted.

The team starts where the platform points, and immediately learns why the count has to run through more than one channel: no single source produces it. The registry export comes back with 216 rows. The platform team adds a population the registry reads differently: agents built in Copilot Studio before the July 2026 identity cutover, which the directory treats as ordinary application registrations rather than agents, as Chapter 5 established. Fifty-eight of those. The automation team is asked next, because Chapter 6's fleet is real here too: 3,100 Power Automate flows, standing delegations running under human credentials, of which 47 call an AI model and act on the result. A one-page survey goes to department heads, worded carefully: how many AI agents or AI-driven automations does your team use, whether or not anyone approved them? The survey surfaces 21 tools, 14 of them appearing in no other channel, including a contract-review service the legal department has been paying for on a corporate card. Procurement records add two more vendor subscriptions with tenant data access that nobody in the survey mentioned, presumably because nobody in the survey knew. The reconciled total is 337, and the team records it as a floor, not a census: departments misread survey questions, and tools bought on cards hide in expense codes procurement was never going to read. A first pass undercounts. Its job is to exist.

Then the team goes looking for the other number, and this is the step that changes the exercise from inventory into governance. The company's AI working group has been meeting monthly for two years; its minutes record 44 approvals. Matching the 44 to the 337 turns out to be its own project, because tenants drift: display names change, agents get repurposed and inherited across reorganizations, and the item the minutes approved as Underwriting FAQ now runs in the tenant as UW Assist v3, doing somewhat more than answering questions. Every discovered agent gets a catalog entry recording what it is, where it was found, who deployed it, and whether any authorization stands behind it, and every entry lands in one of three conditions: approved and governed, approved but ungoverned, or never approved at all. The categories will be argued; somebody will point to a vendor contract or a general technology policy as the approval nobody wrote down per agent. The catalog's discipline is that approval status is answered by producing a named artifact and a named person, and an approval that cannot be produced is filed as absent, however sincerely it is remembered. The third population is the largest. It usually is, and it is worth repeating the framework library's observation about who builds it: shadow agents are not the work of rogue employees. They are the work of motivated employees using exactly the tools they were given.

Three hundred thirty-seven entries cannot all be governed at once, and the objection arrives on schedule, in the head of operational risk's own staff meeting: we cannot write authorization documents for three hundred agents. The answer is that nobody asked for three hundred documents this quarter. The team tiers the catalog by what each agent can reach and do. Agents that only read internal, non-sensitive material sit at the bottom. Agents that touch regulated data or feed human decisions sit in the middle. Agents that communicate externally, move money, write to systems of record, or invoke other agents sit at the top, and there are eleven of those, which is a very manageable number of things to govern first. Chapter 11 made the underlying point about proportionality, and it bears one restating in inventory terms: the tiering is the first page of the record, not a delay of it.

Remediation follows the tiers, and the vocabulary here matters more than it appears to. An unapproved agent at the bottom tier gets documented. An unapproved agent at the top tier gets a decision, made now, by someone with authority: authorize it, with a written scope and a named owner and a review date, or suspend it until someone will. What no agent gets is a backdated blessing. A document written this quarter cannot authorize last year's operation, and pretending otherwise converts the record from an authorization into an explanation, which is the genre of document examiners are paid to see through. Nothing forbids writing the explanation; legal may well want a ratification memo in the file, and it can sit there under its own name. The discipline is the label. The record states what was decided, when, by whom, and the gap between deployment and decision stays visible in it, because the gap is a fact and the file is a record of facts.

The last movement is the one that determines whether the quarter's work survives the year. The catalog gets an intake gate: new agents enter production through it or not at all, and the gate is designed to be easier to use than to route around, because a gate that loses on convenience loses, period. The catalog gets maintenance triggers: an owner departs, a scope changes, a business process moves, and the affected entries come up for review. And the catalog gets read, which sounds too obvious to print until you watch what happens otherwise. Twelve months on, in this same insurer, an internal auditor pulls the ownership history of one top-tier agent and finds it has changed hands four times in eleven months, maker to manager to a transferred manager to a team lead who has since resigned, each handoff executed cleanly by the machinery Chapter 2 watched work at machine speed, and not one accompanied by any review of what the agent was doing or whether its scope still held. The catalog recorded every handoff. Its only reader was the process that wrote it.

## From count to ratio

The reconciliation produces a catalog, and the catalog produces something an executive can actually be held to: two numbers and their relationship. How many agents operate in the environment. What fraction of them carries the full set of governance artifacts, meaning an authorization record on file, an accountable owner who was told and accepted, evidence that somebody reviewed the agent before it went live, and a review date that has not expired. Divide the second population by the first and the result is a coverage ratio. The insurer's arithmetic is unflattering: of 337 agents operating, 29 carry all four artifacts, a shade under nine percent, a figure the CRO is now in a position to report accurately, which is more than most of the company's peers can say. And the figure is not a one-time disclosure. It gets recomputed on a calendar, and it moves, because agents arrive faster than approvals and review dates expire quietly. A denominator that climbs while the numerator stands still is not housekeeping. It is a finding, arriving early enough to be cheap.

The ratio is only as honest as its denominator, which is why the counting rule has to be written down before anyone counts. What counts as an agent, for this purpose: anything deployed that can act, autonomously or semi-autonomously, on the strength of an AI model's output, which sweeps in the Copilot Studio and Foundry populations, the model-calling flows, and the third-party tools with access to organizational data. A raw model deployment with no path to action is a model, not an agent. Ephemeral sub-agents spawned at runtime count through the orchestration that spawned them, not individually, unless the organization has granted a spawned agent standing identity and authority of its own, at which point it has earned its own row. An organization is free to draw these lines differently, provided the definition is written and applied consistently, because the first question anyone competent will ask about a ratio is what was counted. An unwritten definition makes the ratio fiction, and a definition that changes between quarters makes it fiction with a methodology section.

The counting boundary is not a governance exemption, and one adjacent population proves the point. Consequential AI systems that are not agents, the scoring engines and rankers and underwriting models that inform decisions without taking actions, carry the same authorization requirements and belong in a parallel inventory with the same four artifacts, stated for systems that inform decisions rather than take them, and a coverage ratio of their own, reported beside the agent ratio rather than blended into it. Some systems will appear on both lists, an agent on one and the scoring model it calls on the other, and the two entries should name each other, because the examiner who finds one will ask for the other. Chapter 9 showed why the two lists must both exist and stay distinct: the bank's compliance team went looking for a missing approval in its model inventory and came back empty, because the deployment had never crossed the threshold of anything that list was built to notice. An organization that reports a clean agent ratio while its consequential models run ungoverned has not closed its gap. It has relocated it to the list nobody asked about yet.

One more boundary moved in August 2026. Reconciliation assumes you know which tenants to reconcile, and Microsoft Entra Tenant Governance, generally available since August 10, 2026, now surfaces the ones your organization never knew it had: related tenants detected from B2B traffic, shared billing, and multitenant applications, shadow tenants included, with configuration drift monitored across six services (Microsoft Entra blog, August 10, 2026; Microsoft Learn, Tenant Governance overview, verified

August 13, 2026). Read it as this chapter one layer up. The platform can now prove which tenants exist and how they drift. It still holds no record of what any agent inside them was authorized to do, and a tenant nobody governs holds agents nobody counts.

Plotted together, the two numbers place an organization on a simple map, and the map has a name: the Governance Readiness Matrix, one axis for how many AI systems actually operate and one for the fraction verifiably covered. High count and high coverage is the destination, governed at scale, occupied by a small minority who built the intake gate before they needed it. Low count and high coverage is discipline before scale. Low count and low coverage is the pilot phase, safe exactly as long as the pilots stay small and the governance gets built first. High count and low coverage is where most enterprises sit in 2026, and this book has been using its name as a common noun all along: agent sprawl. The quadrant names are mnemonics; the substance an organization reports is the two numbers underneath them. The matrix asks nothing an examiner would not ask. It only asks it earlier, on your own calendar, at your own desk, while the answer can still be improved rather than defended. And it comes with a built-in placement test: an organization that cannot compute its ratio at all, because it lacks one of the two numbers, has learned its position anyway. The missing number is the finding.

Which returns the chapter to the federal department with the 33,000 hours, because those hours have a precise anatomy. They were not spent patching; patching is fast. They were spent discovering, system by system, under emergency conditions, a list that could have existed in advance, and the department's misfortune was only that its forcing event arrived before its inventory did. Your organization's agent estate is accumulating toward its own forcing event, whether that event is an examiner's request list, an incident postmortem, or an audit committee's one-line question, and on that day the running count will render in seconds, exported from a console, timestamped and complete. The platform counts the agents. Only you can count the approvals.

---

**Where an organization actually sits**

| | Coverage high | Coverage low |
|---|---|---|
| **Count low** | Discipline ahead of scale | The pilot phase, which holds only while the pilots stay small |
| **Count high** | The gate went up before it was needed | Agent sprawl, where most enterprises sit |

*Four labels, two numbers. The labels are shorthand; the numbers are what gets reported. An organization that cannot compute the ratio has still learned its position, because the absent number is the finding.*

*The matrix is diagnostic, not aspirational. An organization's position is established by evidence it can produce today, not by the program it has funded.*

# Chapter 15

# Authorization Coverage Lifecycle Across Microsoft Tools

The lawsuit began with a birthday.

In 2022, the United States Equal Employment Opportunity Commission sued iTutorGroup, a company that hired tutors in the United States to teach English online, alleging that its application software had been programmed to automatically reject female applicants aged fifty-five and older and male applicants aged sixty and older. No human saw the rejected applications. More than two hundred people were turned away by rule, on arrival, for the year of birth on the form (EEOC v. iTutorGroup, Inc., No. 1:22-cv-2565, E.D.N.Y.). The company settled: agreement filed August 9, 2023, consent decree approved September 8, 2023, 365,000 dollars for the affected applicants and five years of EEOC monitoring. The Commission's chair had made the position plain when the agency filed suit: automating the discrimination does not move the responsibility off the employer.

Hold the mechanics of detection up to the light, because they are the part of this case your organization should find uncomfortable. The rejection rule did not drift into the software, and there was no opaque model whose reasoning anyone would have needed to reconstruct. Someone wrote an ordinary rule, which means it sat in the configuration from the beginning, in plain text, discoverable by any review that ever compared what the system was doing against what anyone would be willing to defend. No such review ever ran. What exposed the rule instead was one rejected applicant who resubmitted the same application with a more recent date of birth and promptly received an interview offer. Two records, one changed field, opposite outcomes. It was a clean controlled experiment, the exact comparison a scheduled review would have performed, and the only such review the system ever received was conducted, unpaid, by a person it had just rejected.

That is the shape of the problem this chapter is about, and notice that it is not a detection problem. Nothing needed to be caught in the act. The evidence was stationary. What was missing was a calendar: a date on which someone was obligated to look, and a definition of the events that would force a look sooner. The software ran until an outsider audited it by accident. Now ask the version of the question that belongs to your tenant. Every agent running in it was approved, if it was approved at all, by a signature on a specific date, against the configuration and the business as they stood on that date. What, since then, has been scheduled to look?

## The distance no alarm measures

iTutorGroup is the blunt case, wrong from the first execution and merely waiting for a reader. The commoner case is quieter and harder to see, because on the day the approval was signed, the record was accurate. Then the world it described kept moving. Inputs shift. Users learn what else the thing can do and start asking. An upstream data source changes shape. A workflow that consumed the agent's output as a convenience begins depending on it as a step. Nothing fails loudly. The behavior stays near enough to normal that no ticket gets filed, and moves far enough from the approved purpose that the record no longer describes what is running. The agent has not left its technical boundary. The boundary was never the purpose.

A lending company priced this distance in public. Upstart Holdings launched Model 22, a new iteration of its AI underwriting system, in May 2025, presenting it to investors as the engine behind rising approval rates. Through the third quarter of 2025 the model responded to upticks in macroeconomic signals by tightening credit, and the company's conversion rate fell from 23.9 percent in the second quarter to 20.6 percent in the third. On the November 4, 2025 earnings call, management described the model as overly responsive to recent signals and acknowledged calibrating it to run more conservatively during the quarter; full-year revenue guidance came down by twenty million dollars, and the stock fell 9.71 percent the next day. A securities class action followed in April 2026, alleging investors should have been told sooner (Dunn v. Upstart Holdings, Inc., No. 3:26-cv-02974, N.D. Cal., filed April 7, 2026; the allegations are allegations, and no court has ruled on the merits). Set the securities question aside, because it belongs to the litigation. The governance fact sits outside the dispute: a production model's behavior moved away from the purpose its owners believed it was serving, quarter by quarter, and the instrument that finally measured the movement was the earnings call. Model risk monitoring watched the model. The income statement is what published the finding. Whether anything inside the company measured the distance sooner, and what happened if it did, are questions the docket will settle; what the public record shows is which instrument made the distance undeniable.

The industry has a name for this distance: the Intent Gap, the space between the purpose an organization approved and the behavior its system is exhibiting in production today. The term earns its place in this book for one structural reason. Governance records are static and production is not, so the gap opens by default, silently, unless something is built to measure it. And almost nothing an enterprise already monitors will measure it. Access reviews recertify who can reach the system. Uptime dashboards confirm it is running. Cost reports confirm it is being used, often more than anyone projected, which is read as success. Every one of those instruments can stay green while the answer to "is this still doing what we approved it to do" quietly becomes no. Chapter 4 caught one mechanism in a single line: an approval that silently extends to whatever appears after the signature is a subscription, and the tenant amends the subscription daily. Chapter 13 caught another at the enforcement layer, where whatever nobody labeled rides the default. Different mechanisms, one geometry. The record holds still while the thing it describes moves, and the organization that only watches activity will learn about the distance the way Upstart's investors did, from the consequences.

## Three phases, one ratio

Watch what organizations actually do about this, and a pattern repeats reliably enough to name its stages.

In the first phase, agents are being deployed faster than anyone is writing anything down. Each team's deployment is individually reasonable, most of the builders were never told a governance step was expected of them, and the debt accrues invisibly because nobody is computing it. The recognizable tells are mundane. There is no intake step a new agent must pass through. The count of agents produced by IT and the count produced by the business units disagree, and no one has reconciled them. The AI policy, where it exists, states principles rather than requirements with checkpoints. Ask who is accountable for the aggregate posture and the answer is a committee, which is a name shared widely enough to belong to no one.

The second phase begins on the day the gap acquires a name inside the building, and the day is rarely chosen. A regulator asks for the list. An incident involves an agent with more reach than anyone remembered granting. A board member asks a question the existing documentation cannot answer. Now the organization knows, and it is measuring, usually for the first time, and it is in reactive mode: ownership being assigned to agents already live, reviews being run because of the specific event rather than as a standing gate, and explanations being drafted for deployments that predate the process. Chapter 11 already gave that last artifact its correct name, and one clause carries it here: a document written after the fact explains; it does not authorize.

In the third phase the machinery finally points forward. An intake process exists and is actually enforced, including for the deployments described as urgent, which is where enforcement is usually tested first. New agents cannot go live ungoverned by default, so the debt stops compounding while the backlog is worked. The accountable executive can state the coverage number, its direction, and the remediation priorities without a two-week evidence hunt. And the cultural tell, which is worth more than any metric: when a team proposes a new agent, its first question is what the intake requires, not who can grant the exemption.

The Authorization Coverage Lifecycle is the name this book's framework library gives the three phases, and the framework's working test is the ratio the previous chapter built: governed agents over total agents, both counts produced by the written rule, recomputed on a calendar. The ratio is the placement instrument, and placement is the point, because self-assessment fails here in one direction only. Organizations place themselves by intention, and intentions all sound like phase three. The ratio places them by evidence. An organization drafting an intake process that has never intercepted a deployment is in the second phase however advanced its slideware; an organization with a policy and no measurement is still in the first. The distance between where the organization believes it stands and where its ratio puts it is not a preliminary to the finding. It is the finding, and it is the cheapest one an examiner will ever get to write, because the organization's own numbers write it.

## What forces the review

Every driver on the road holds the answer to this chapter in their wallet. A driving credential is not a lifetime grant; the state that issued it printed an expiry date on its face, and beyond the calendar it defined the events that force an earlier look: a medical episode, an age threshold, enough violations. Nobody considers this insulting to drivers. The 1998 road test proved what the driver could do in 1998, and the state declines to extend that proof indefinitely on faith. The authorization record for an agent needs exactly this pair of mechanisms, a date it expires and a list of events that reopen it early, and the second mechanism is where the organizational design work actually lives, because the calendar is easy and the event list is a set of decisions nobody has been assigned to make.

Start with the events the platform will happily perform without ever raising the question. A new connector gets consented, in Copilot Studio or Power Platform, and the agent's reach extends into a system the original approval never mentioned. A flow adds the agent as an action and the agent acquires a caller. An identity migration or a registry onboarding rolls through and every field carries over into the new scheme, correct, current, and continuous. It is worth being precise about that last one, because the paperwork it generates feels like governance. Re-registration is filing. The directory's records about the agent get newer; the organization's decision about the agent does not. A migration that moves an agent into a new identity model asks whether the fields map, not whether the scope still holds, and an approval does not become current by being copied forward. The migration did its job, which was preserving configuration; deciding whether the preserved scope deserved to survive the move was never on its checklist. Any of these events can be defined as a review trigger. None is a trigger by default: the platform records the event and routes it nowhere, because the routing is your construction, and there is no negligence in that; it cannot see your approval, so it cannot know which changes amend it.

Then there are the events the platform cannot see at all, and the most important one in most tenants is a threshold crossing that changes no configuration whatsoever. An agent built for one person's convenience starts feeding a department's process. The maker's Monday-morning summary becomes the input to the team's Monday-morning meeting, then to a report a manager signs. Nothing in any log marks the day that happened, because what changed was reliance, not settings, and Chapter 5 left the resulting question deliberately open: at what point does a personal tool require departmental authorization? The lifecycle answer is that the point must be defined in advance as a trigger, in writing, in terms a business owner can apply. Output leaves the maker's own inbox. A second team takes a dependency. The agent's product reaches a customer or a regulator. Pick the definition and enforce it, but pick it, because this is the one trigger only the organization is positioned to fire, and the crossing it marks is where a convenience becomes a liability with a blast radius.

Ownership events belong on the list for a reason now visible from three angles. When an agent's human sponsor leaves, the directory can reassign the field at machine speed, and Chapter 2 established what that reassignment carries in the way of decision, which is nothing. The identity-governance attestation machinery

Chapter 8 conceded can then reconfirm the new name on a faithful cadence, and what it binds that name to is whatever scope document exists, which is frequently none. Here is the lifecycle reading of both facts: the platform has supplied the reminder system and left the substance of the reminder to you. An owner-departure trigger that routes the agent into an actual re-authorization, scope reread, risk reaccepted, name signed, converts the attestation from a field ceremony into a review. And the quieter cousin of the departure problem is the automation that no longer notices departures at all. Chapter 6 showed the machinery that once forced a look, the failure prompt on a departed employee's connection, being engineered away in the name of resilience. Service-principal ownership is fully governable, and nothing about it schedules its own governance. The healthier the plumbing, the more deliberate the calendar has to be, because nothing will break on its own to demand attention, and this only compounds: governance surfaces will keep arriving on the platform side, and none of them will be a feature designed to fail so that somebody looks. An outage is not a review plan. The same discipline extends down the chain: dedicated agent identities, service-principal connection ownership, and the maker-credential controls with their documented autonomy costs are each per-agent decisions Chapter 9 found nobody assigned to make, and the lifecycle is where they get an owner and a revisit date, agent by agent, at intake and at every renewal.

Two more trigger classes come from outside the tenant. Regulatory change is one: when the banking agencies redrew their model risk guidance in April 2026 and excluded generative and agentic AI from its scope while directing institutions to cover the gap themselves (SR 26-2, April 17, 2026), every authorization that leaned on the prior guidance acquired a review obligation, prudential rather than statutory, that no monitoring alert would ever raise. The letter is guidance, not law; what it withdrew was the comfort of pointing at the old one. An incident, anywhere in the chain, is the other, with one sober note attached from Chapter 13's arithmetic: an examination that reaches back through years of an agent's operation will meet audit defaults measured in days, so the review the trigger forces had better produce a record that outlives the logs.

## One renewal, constructed

What the machinery looks like when it runs is worth seeing once at ground level. The scene that follows is constructed, in the manner of this book's earlier exercises, and assembled from parts already on your org chart.

Another regional bank, eleven months ago: a payments-exceptions agent clears intake. The intake record is two pages in the bank's own agent catalog, an artifact the bank built rather than bought, because no platform ships it. Purpose, in the business owner's words. Authorized actions and the prohibitions, which took longer to write than the actions. Data reach, written as the named connectors. A named owner in operations, a named sponsor above her. A review date, set at twelve months because the agent sits in the middle risk tier, and the trigger list, printed on the record itself. In month nine, one of the triggers fires early: the owner resigns. Her departure feeds the review queue automatically, because the bank tied the agent's lifecycle to its people's lifecycle in the identity system, which is to say someone wired the offboarding checklist that human resources already runs into the agent catalog and the wiring took an afternoon.

The renewal meeting runs twenty minutes and the packet has three parts. The original record. The diff: two connectors added since approval under change tickets that referenced the record's identifier, a scheduled Power Automate flow that now calls the agent nightly, volume up fourfold, and one prohibited-action test added to the monitoring after a near miss in March. And the recommendation. The incoming owner reads the scope before the meeting because her name is about to be on it, which concentrates attention in a way no awareness training ever has. The committee re-authorizes with an amended scope covering the flow, or it suspends pending a narrower rebuild. Those are the available verbs. What it does not do is bless the past eleven months retroactively; the record notes the review date, the decision, and the signature, and the archive keeps the prior version, so an examiner reading the file later sees a decision trail rather than a restoration.

Nothing in that scene required new software. The intake form is a form. The diff is an export and a change-ticket query. The queue is a calendar with authority behind it. The expensive part, and the part that distinguishes a phase-three organization from an organization with phase-three ambitions, is that every element had an assigned owner and the meeting actually happened, on schedule, without an incident to justify it.

## The date on the signature

Return once more to the applicant with two records, because her experiment generalizes. She compared the system's behavior against a fact and got an answer in a day. The comparison was always that cheap. What her would-be employer lacked was not the capability to run it but the obligation to, on a date, on a trigger, with a name attached to the result.

Your tenant's oldest authorization has a date on it. Find it, and then list what has changed since that date without any obligation to revisit the signature: the connectors added, the flows attached, the owner turnover, the teams that started depending on the output, the guidance that moved underneath it. Some of that change arrived on Microsoft's own release calendar, capability by capability, default by default, and none of it arrived with a form asking whether your approval still holds. The platform performed all of those changes flawlessly and recorded most of them. It asked your organization about none of them, because it cannot know which changes matter to a decision it has never seen. The approval was signed once. The agent has changed every quarter since.

---

## Three phases, and the marker that distinguishes them

| | What the organization is doing | The recognizable tell | What ends it |
|---|---|---|---|
| **First** | Deploying faster than anyone is writing anything down | No intake step, two disagreeing counts, an AI policy of principles rather than checkpoints, and a committee named as accountable | Something external: a regulator's list, an incident, a board question |
| **Second** | Measuring for the first time, remediating reactively | Ownership assigned to agents already live, reviews run because of the event rather than as a standing gate | Intake starts intercepting deployments before they ship |
| **Third** | Preventing new debt faster than it accumulates | The ratio is declining and can be reported without preparation | Nothing. This phase is maintained or it is lost. |

*The gap between where an organization believes it sits and where its coverage ratio places it is itself a governance finding.*

## Chapter 16

# The Disposition Protocol and Microsoft Signal Sources

The warning arrived before the market opened.

At 8:01 on the morning of August 1, 2012, an internal system at Knight Capital began sending automated email messages to a group of the firm's personnel. The messages referenced the order router and identified an error. Ninety-seven of them went out before the 9:30 opening bell. Nobody acted on them, and the Securities and Exchange Commission's account of that morning explains why in one flat clause: the messages were not designed to be system alerts, and personnel generally did not review them when they were received. The signal existed. It had an inbox. What it did not have was a single person obligated to read it and a single sentence anywhere in writing about what reading it would require.

The cause sat on one server. Knight had deployed new routing code to eight servers and a technician had missed the eighth, which still carried a function retired in 2003 whose activation flag the new code had repurposed. When the market opened, orders reaching that server woke the old code, which sent child orders into the market without counting the fills. Over the next forty-five minutes the router pushed millions of orders, executing over four million trades in 154 stocks. Knight's own people were watching by then, diagnosing in real time, and in the middle of the diagnosis they made the response that the absence of a written procedure invites: they rolled the new code back off the seven servers that had it right, which spread the defect to all eight. By the time the orders stopped, the firm held roughly 3.5 billion dollars it had not meant to buy and 3.15 billion it had not meant to sell, and the eventual loss exceeded 460 million dollars. Forty-five minutes, start to finish.

The Commission's order arrived on October 16, 2013, the first enforcement action under the Market Access Rule, and it reads less like a description of a coding error than an inventory of absences. The penalty attached to the controls, not the bug. The order faults what was missing in writing: risk controls reasonably designed for the firm's market access, and procedures to guide the response when technology went wrong. And on the ninety-seven emails, the SEC's language is worth keeping intact, because it is the whole subject of this chapter in thirteen words: the messages "provided an opportunity to identify and fix the problem before the markets opened."

An opportunity. Not an obligation. The distance between those two words is where the forty-five minutes lived.

## The settlement that wrote the protocol

Thirteen years later, a state regulator put the same distance in a court filing, this time about an AI system, and this time the remedy is the interesting part.

On July 10, 2025, Massachusetts Attorney General Andrea Joy Campbell announced a 2.5 million dollar settlement with Earnest Operations LLC, a student loan company, resolving allegations that its lending practices, including its AI underwriting models, violated consumer protection and fair lending laws. The allegations, which Earnest denies, run from a model input that produced disparate outcomes to a knockout rule keyed to immigration status. But set the conduct allegations aside for a moment and read the governance count, because it describes a familiar shape. The Attorney General alleged that Earnest deployed its models without testing them for disparate impact, and that the policies it did have were not followed. One detail from the filing carries the whole theme. Earnest had a written policy requiring its compliance officer to receive a certification that any new underwriting criterion complied with fair lending policy. According to the state, the compliance officer never received a single such certification from any employee. The channel was designed, documented, and named in policy. Nothing ever moved through it.

Now read what the settlement required Earnest to build, because the assurance of discontinuance filed in Suffolk County Superior Court is, in effect, a response apparatus written by a regulator for an organization that had not written its own. An internal algorithmic oversight team, with an appointed chairperson responsible for its work. A process by which anyone in the company can report a concern about algorithmic bias without repercussions, and a process by which the team must respond when they do. Annual fair lending testing on a schedule, plus a defined list of trigger events that force testing sooner: a model update, a new model, a credible internal complaint, a change in regulatory guidance. Documentation of every algorithmic underwriting decision, retained for four years. A named steward accountable for the testing, inventory, and documentation of the automatic decline rules.

Look at the grammar of those terms. A named chair. A defined trigger. A required response. A retention period. A steward. The state did not order a better model. It ordered the machinery that converts a signal about the model into a decision about the model, and it specified that machinery in the register regulators reserve for things they have stopped assuming organizations will build voluntarily. Every element of it could have been written internally, years earlier, in an afternoon, by the company's own compliance function, without a dollar of the settlement attached. The organization that writes this document before deployment is doing nothing exotic. It is drafting, on its own letterhead, the paragraphs a regulator will otherwise draft on theirs.

## Six requirements, forty-five minutes

The framework library this book draws on gives that document a name, the Disposition Protocol, and a precise scope: six requirements, written down before the system ships and attached to its authorization record, that turn a detection signal into a governance decision with a document behind it. Detection tells the organization something is happening. The protocol specifies what detection formally requires. The cleanest way to see why there are six, and why each one exists, is to walk them back through Knight's morning, because each requirement is the written answer to a question that morning asked and nobody had prepared.

The first requirement is an Accuracy Owner: one person, carried in the authorization record by name and by role, formally required to receive each accuracy signal, and the owner of whatever decision follows it. Knight's ninety-seven emails went to a group. A group is where a signal goes to be seen by everyone and owned by no one, and the record shows exactly that: received generally, reviewed by nobody, because review was nobody's stated job. The owner requirement is not about creating a bottleneck. It is about creating the one inbox where an unread warning becomes a specific person's unread warning, which is a different and more motivating category of object.

The second is a Trigger Threshold: a number, fixed in writing before launch, past which the owner is no longer weighing a concern but formally obligated to open a review. Not a feeling of unease, and not a judgment call made at 8:15 in the morning while the pre-market queue builds. A number, chosen in calm conditions by the same process that authorized the system. Knight's messages were not designed as alerts, which is another way of saying no one had ever decided what volume or category of error would make them one. And the threshold needs a companion, because statistics cover only the case where the numbers move. The harder case is the one where every metric reads normal and the aggregate outcome is something nobody would have approved had they seen it coming.

The protocol handles it with an observed-outcome trigger: any named person on the notification list who sees a result inconsistent with the authorization's intent may open the same formal review a threshold crossing opens, on the same clock, documented the same way. If raising the flag requires first deciding whether you are allowed to, the organization has not built a trigger. It has built a hesitation, and hesitations do not survive contact with a trading morning.

The third is a Suspension Authority: one named person, distinct from the Accuracy Owner, holding written authority to pause the system while the review runs. Knight had people with the technical power to intervene, which is how the rollback happened. Power to act and authority to act are different assets, and the forty-five minutes were governed by the first in the absence of the second: capable engineers improvising consequential moves under pressure, with no document telling anyone who could order the router out of the market or on what basis. If locating the person with authority to pause a production system takes a meeting to schedule, the pause will lose the race to whatever the system is doing, every time. For the multi-agent chains Chapter 9 examined, the requirement extends one step: the authority must cover the chain as a composition, with a written order of shutdown, because pausing one agent mid-chain leaves the others running on stale handoffs.

The fourth is a Re-Authorization Standard: what must be demonstrated, in evidence, before the system resumes. Root cause identified, root cause addressed, fix validated, clearance documented. The standard is written before deployment for one reason, visible in Knight's rollback. Decisions about a paused or misbehaving system get made under the loudest business pressure the organization ever generates, and a standard assembled in that moment will be exactly as rigorous as the pressure permits. Written in advance, it is the one voice in the room with no interest in the next fifteen minutes.

The fifth is a Notification Clock: a list of who must be told and a maximum window for telling them, starting when the threshold is crossed, not when the incident closes. Counsel, the risk committee of the board, the regulatory liaison, whoever the organization has determined holds a right to know. The clock exists to keep notice from becoming a cleanup task performed after the narrative is settled. The people on the list acquire the right to know at the moment the trigger fires, because that is when the governance process began, whether or not anyone chooses to run it.

The sixth is a Decision Window: a deadline by which a formal decision, hold, resume, or escalate, is documented, and a default action that executes automatically if the window closes without one. The default is itself a design decision with tiers: where an abrupt halt would do damage of its own, a payments chain caught mid-settlement, the written default can be escalation alone, with a named human making any stop, and that tiering lives in the same record. Knight never defined a decision window, so the market defined one. Forty-five minutes, non-negotiable, enforced by capital.

That is the whole protocol: an owner, a threshold, a pause authority, a restart standard, a clock, and a deadline, each one a sentence or two in an authorization record, each one answering a question Knight's morning asked at a cost of just over ten million dollars a minute.

## What the tenant already hears

Map this onto a Microsoft estate and the first discovery is encouraging, briefly. The detection layer the protocol depends on is not something you need to build. Much of it is already firing.

The signals arrive in two categories, and the difference between them matters more than any individual capability. The first category is tenant-level: signals the platform generates and routes to consoles your security organization already staffs. Purview's audit surface records agent interactions and its data-security posture views raise alerts, on the terms, tiers, and scoping Chapter 13 priced. Microsoft Defender raises security detections. Microsoft Entra logs every agent sign-in, and since the identity work Chapter 12 walked through, it marks agent activity as agent activity, filterable as its own class. These signals share a property that makes them easy to mistake for governance: they arrive whether or not anyone asked for them. Enable the licensing, and the console fills. A CISO reading this can reasonably say the detection layer is the platform's best half, and the CISO is right.

The second category is nothing like that. The Agent Governance Toolkit, which Microsoft released as open source on April 2, 2026 under an MIT license, is a runtime policy engine that engineering teams adopt deliberately, through SDKs, inside agent code they build. Where a team has instrumented it, it intercepts agent actions against policy at runtime and writes an audit trail of what it intercepted. Enforcement is the toolkit's first job; the audit trail is the byproduct, and the byproduct is what this chapter cares about. Where a team has not, it produces nothing, because it is not there. Its evidence is developer-adopted, per-agent, and exactly as uneven as your engineering organization's practices. The presence of toolkit logs in one agent's record proves that one team's discipline. It proves nothing about the tenant, and its absence from another agent's record was not a decision anyone made. It was a sprint that ended.

Watch one signal travel. The scene is constructed, and labeled as such, assembled from surfaces prior chapters have already verified. A Copilot Studio agent at another mid-sized insurer, built to summarize policy renewals, begins quoting from a library of claims files it had never touched, and a data-security alert fires on the sensitive-content access, exactly as designed. The alert lands in the console the security team staffs. The analyst who triages it finds no malware, no exfiltration, no violation with a severity attached, and closes it as informational, which is the correct answer to the question the console asks. Nobody asks the other question, whether the agent's authorization covered the new library, because that question belongs to no console, and the person who would have owned it was never named. The Copilot admins could suspend the agent in a minute. Nothing requires them to, and it is not their call. Six sentences in an authorization record would have made it somebody's.

Keep the two categories separate in your mental model, because they fail differently. Tenant-level signals are broad and nobody owns them; they land in consoles staffed for security triage, not for authorization review, and an accuracy drift that trips no security rule swims past them entirely. Developer-adopted evidence is deep and nobody mandates it; it exists just where your most conscientious teams already were, which is the inverse of where governance risk concentrates. And both categories share the Knight property, the one the SEC named in thirteen words. Every signal in every console is an opportunity. The platform routes information. It sets no threshold, names no owner, starts no clock, and enforces no deadline, because those are decisions about your obligations, and the platform has never seen your obligations. Your tenant is already generating its ninety-seven emails. The open question is the same one Knight's inbox posed, and it is not a question about detection.

## The third kind of ending

There is a second class of signal the consoles will never raise, and it is the one most likely to reach your desk first: the signals that arrive as ordinary corporate events rather than alerts.

Chapter 7 watched a city's chatbot leave production and noted what the record showed: agents end through an incident or through a budget line, and the third kind of ending, a governance decision, requires an artifact most agents never get. The Disposition Protocol is where the third ending becomes available, because a governance decision about a running system needs the machinery the six requirements install: someone empowered to stop it, a standard for what resuming requires, and a window in which deciding is mandatory. Without them, the organization can want to decide and still find that no one, on any given Tuesday, is actually required to.

Watch how the commonest quiet signal plays out without the protocol. An agent's owner resigns. The previous chapter treated the departure as a review trigger, an event that routes the agent into a scheduled re-authorization, and that is the right lifecycle answer. But there is a disposition question inside the event that cannot wait for the review queue: what is the agent's status during the gap? It is running right now, ownerless, and running-while-ownerless is a state somebody should have to choose. The platform's best process for the moment, the orphaned-object handling Chapter 6 examined, offers a menu of ownership dispositions, reassign it, take it over, delete it, and carries no authorization question in any option. The tooling can transfer the agent to a new name in minutes, and the practical effect is an agent whose builder left in March still writing to production in July, under a fresh owner name and the original, unexamined scope. Whether the agent should be operating at all between the resignation and the review is a decision the menu does not contain, and in the tenant without a protocol, the answer is supplied by default: it keeps running, because continuing is what happens when stopping is nobody's call to make.

That default has a shape you have seen twice now in real records. Earnest's certification channel, formally designed and never used. Knight's ninety-seven messages, generated and unread. The absence being described is not detection and it is not even attention. It is the standing, written answer to a signal, and in its absence every signal, however loud, is converted into the organization's ambient noise at the speed of a forwarded email.

## The drill

The sequence that performs the conversion is worth printing once, because every reader has watched it run. An URGENT email becomes a status update. The status update becomes a Thursday agenda item. The agenda item becomes an action item. The action item produces no decision. The system keeps running.

Nothing in that sequence is negligence. Every step is a reasonable person doing a reasonable thing with a signal that arrived without an obligation attached, and that is precisely the problem, because the sequence is what organizations do with information by default, and detection produces information. Only a written protocol produces anything else.

Every commercial building your organization occupies already runs the model this chapter is describing. The alarm on the wall is detection, and nobody confuses installing it with being prepared. The preparation is the drill: the written, rehearsed answer to what every person in the building must do when the alarm sounds, who calls, who sweeps the floor, who is authorized to declare the building clear for re-entry. The alarm without the drill is noise, and the building code does not permit the combination, because a century of fires taught the inspectors what a decade of AI deployments is now teaching the regulators: the alarm was never the hard part.

Your tenant's alarms are installed and sounding. Purview logged something last week that touched an agent whose authorization record, if it exists, does not say who was required to look. Out in the estate an agent is running under an owner who has resigned, or a threshold nobody set, or a suspension authority that would take a meeting to locate. The six sentences that would change this are not waiting on a product release, a budget cycle, or a standards body. They are waiting to be written, and until they are, every console in the estate is delivering opportunities to an organization that has assigned itself no obligations. The alert fired on time. Nothing in writing said what had to happen next.

**Six things decided before deployment, or decided under pressure**

| The part | What it fixes in advance | What the platform does | What the platform cannot do |
|---|---|---|---|
| The accuracy owner | One named person who receives every signal and owns what happens next | Routes the alert | Assign the human obligation to act on it |
| The trigger threshold | A number, written before deployment, at which concern becomes formal review | Surfaces the metric | Choose the number |
| The suspension authority | A second name, not the first, who can halt production alone | Executes the pause | Decide the pause is required |
| The re-authorization standard | What must be demonstrated before the system resumes | Records the restart | Define what makes restart defensible |
| The notification clock | Who has a right to know, and the maximum hours before they are told | Sends and preserves the notice | Decide who has a right to know |
| The decision window | A deadline for hold, resume, or escalate, and the default if it closes | Timestamps the trigger and tracks elapsed time | Enforce the deadline |

*Each row is a decision. Leave one unmade and it will be made anyway, under pressure, by whoever is in the room when the threshold is crossed.*

Chapter 17

# The Agent Governance Toolkit and What It Cannot Prove

On May 14, 2026, Microsoft published a blog post titled "After the Agent Acts: Proving What Happened and Who Authorized It." Sit with that title, because it is not a marketing headline. It is the seven questions from Chapter 1, compressed by a vendor's own engineering team into eleven words.

The post is the third in a series. Part one, published in April, walked through runtime governance: a policy engine that intercepts a tool call before it executes, a zero-trust identity layer for agents talking to other agents, execution sandboxing that keeps one agent's failure from becoming everyone's. Part two, in early May, walked through shift-left governance: pull request gates, attestation checklists, supply-chain checks that catch a bad dependency before it ships. Both parts answer a real engineering question competently. Neither one is the question this book has been asking. Then, in part three, Microsoft's own engineers wrote the sentence sixteen chapters have been building toward. No policy engine, they note, prevents a past action. No shift-left gate reconstructs a delegation chain after the fact. No tool tells an auditor whether the identity that authorized a trade was legitimately derived from a human principal or injected somewhere mid-chain. Microsoft names this itself, in its own post, as a gap that "neither runtime enforcement nor pre-runtime checks were designed to answer."

This book did not hand Microsoft that sentence. Seven weeks earlier, on March 24, 2026, a newsletter with a few dozen subscribers had drawn the same line in different words: an audit trail shows the action, not the decision; a system can be configured without ever being authorized. Microsoft's engineers arrived at their version of the same insight independently, from inside a production codebase rather than a newsletter, answering questions their own customers kept asking. Two people noticing the same missing floorboard from different rooms of the house is corroboration, not a priority dispute. And corroboration from the vendor selling the platform is worth more to a skeptical CISO than corroboration from anyone selling a book about the vendor's platform.

So this chapter does something different from the chapters before it. It takes Microsoft's own most sophisticated answer to the authorization question seriously, credits it in full, and then shows exactly where the answer stops being an answer.

## What the kernel actually does

Start with what deserves the credit, because most of it is real engineering against a real problem.

The Agent Governance Toolkit, released as open source under the MIT license on April 2, 2026, works on a simple architectural bet: prompt-level safety is probabilistic, and probabilistic security is not security. An agent politely asked not to run a destructive command can still be talked into running it, the way any sufficiently persuasive conversation can talk a person into most things. The toolkit's answer is to stop asking. Every tool call an agent routes through the governance kernel, every message it sends to another agent, every delegation from an orchestrator to a sub-agent, gets intercepted in deterministic code before the model's output reaches anything that can act on it. That qualifier matters and this book will keep restating it: the toolkit governs what is wired through it, not everything an agent could ever do on a tenant it has credentials for. A policy file written in YAML declares what is allowed, and the kernel enforces it the way an operating system enforces a permission boundary: not as a recommendation, but as a wall. An agent instructed to read a customer record and summarize it cannot also drop a database table, not because it was told not to, but because the action never reaches the interpreter that would run it. That is a genuine advance over the alternative, which is a system prompt and hope.

Around that enforcement core sit three more pieces, all shipped, all real. An identity layer gives every agent a cryptographic identity, distinct from the identities of the humans and services around it, with a named human sponsor attached at creation and a cascade-revocation behavior that kills every downstream delegation the moment the root identity is revoked, rather than requiring someone to hunt sub-agents one at a time. An execution sandbox isolates what an agent can reach, containing a compromised or malfunctioning agent the way a shipping container contains whatever is inside it, whether or not the contents are labeled correctly. And an audit layer logs every governance decision, every allow and every deny, into a hash-chained record designed to be tamper-evident: alter one entry and the chain breaks visibly, the same principle a notary's sequential page numbering has used for centuries, rendered in cryptography instead of ink. The toolkit maps its own coverage against the OWASP Top 10 for Agentic Applications, the risk taxonomy the security community published in December 2025, and by the toolkit's own published mapping it carries full coverage on seven of the ten categories and partial coverage, by its own honest labeling, on the remaining three. That is still a serious claim. It is also a claim written by the people who built the thing being graded, and a CISO reading it should treat "partial" as an invitation to ask what "partial" covers before writing it into a compliance narrative.

One dated note, because this surface moves faster than any other in the book: the OWASP risk list the toolkit maps itself against has already been renamed once since the toolkit shipped, from the Agentic Top 10 to an Agentic Security Initiative taxonomy with new category numbers, with the toolkit's own package keeping the old numbering as a backward-compatible alias so nothing breaks in the meantime. A capability chapter written in this space has a shelf life measured in months, not years, and this one is dated on that basis: as of mid-2026.

None of this is vaporware, and none of it is trivial. A production system that structurally cannot execute an unapproved destructive command, with a tamper-evident record of every decision it made along the way, is more agent governance than the overwhelming majority of enterprises running agents today have anywhere in their environment. An examiner who found this instrumented and running would, correctly, take it as evidence of a serious governance posture. It is the single most credible technical answer to "can you prove what the agent did" on the Microsoft stack, in any chapter.

One boundary needs stating plainly before going further: the toolkit is framework-level infrastructure, distributed as packages for Python, TypeScript, Rust, Go, and .NET, that a development team wires into the code they are writing. It is not a Copilot Studio feature, and it does not arrive by osmosis because an organization licenses Microsoft 365 Copilot or builds agents through the low-code studio. A tenant can run Copilot Studio agents by the thousand and never touch this toolkit at all. Where it applies is where a developer building on Azure AI Foundry, or on Microsoft Agent Framework, chose to bring it in.

Which is exactly why the next question matters more than any capability list. Proving what the agent did was never the hard part. Chapter 1 made that distinction on page one, and nothing in this toolkit moves it.

## The button that looks like the answer

The toolkit ships a policy type called *require_approval.* Configure it, and a defined action, deleting a record, sending funds, writing to production, routes to a named human before it executes. The policy can require more than one approver and a time limit on the wait.

Read the code sample cold, and it looks like the missing piece: a human, in the loop, before the consequential action, on the record.

It is the closest thing on the Microsoft stack to an authorization surface at agent-tool-call runtime, and this book should say so plainly rather than wave it away. Be precise about what that phrase covers. Platform-level authorization, who is allowed to configure a policy, grant a scope, or provision an agent identity in the first place, still runs through Entra roles and privileged-access workflows, untouched by anything this chapter describes. The require_approval gate governs the moment an already-built agent tries to act. Nothing in the toolkit's own documentation claims that moment produces an authorization record either. It is a runtime confirmation on a specific action, which is a narrower claim than this book is here to test, and a fair one.

Consider a real-shaped example, constructed to make the point rather than reported from any client engagement. An accounts-payable agent processes vendor payments and updates vendor banking details when a vendor submits a change request. The engineering team, sensibly, put *require_approval* on any wire above fifty thousand dollars, with two approvers and a thirty-minute window. Nobody put the same policy on updating the banking details a payment is sent to, because that action looked administrative rather than financial when the policy file was written. Every dollar that leaves the account now carries a clean, cryptographically signed, two-person approval trail. The routing number those dollars follow was changed by the agent alone, unreviewed, because the person who wrote the YAML was thinking about the size of the transaction and not about the much older fraud pattern that changes where the money goes rather than how much of it leaves. This is not a novel attack. Vendor-account-takeover and business-email-compromise fraud have run this exact play against finance departments for a decade, changing the beneficiary rather than the amount, precisely because the amount is what gets watched. The audit log for that agent will look immaculate in an examination. It will also be missing the one control that would have caught the actual failure mode, and nothing in the toolkit would have flagged the gap, because the toolkit enforces the policy file exactly as written and has no way to know what the file's author forgot to write. The same blind spot travels: a customer-support agent gated on closing an account but not on changing the phone number tied to it, a deployment agent gated on shipping to production but not on rotating the secret that production trusts. The vendor is different every time. The unguarded neighbor is always the field that looked administrative when someone wrote the policy.

But look at what the click actually proves. It proves that a named person, at a specific timestamp, approved this action, in this instance, under this policy. It does not prove that the policy itself was reviewed by anyone entitled to accept the risk it governs. A developer who writes *min_approvals=2* for a destructive database action, and never adds an approval gate anywhere near the same agent's ability to email a customer, has made a scoping decision. Nobody outside that developer's team was asked whether that scoping decision was the right one. The approver clicking "approve" is answering the policy's question, not authoring it. A person can click approve correctly, honestly, and promptly, on a policy that should never have existed in that form, and the toolkit has no way to know the difference.

That is the first of four places where this book has, until now, deliberately reserved judgment, because the honest answer needed the whole toolkit in view. The second is the Agent Control Specification, an open specification within the toolkit that defines checkpoints where a policy verdict can route an action to a human rather than simply allow or block it. Structurally, this is the same argument wearing different clothes: the specification enforces whatever verdict a policy author wrote, and has no opinion on whether the policy itself deserved sign-off. The third is a more general claim that has surfaced in several forms across earlier chapters, that a sufficiently rich platform surface, an instructions field, a policy manifest, a delegation token, can hold the organization's governance intent directly, making a separate authorization record redundant. It cannot, for the same reason a job description cannot substitute for the hiring decision that produced it. The surface carries whatever was written into it, faithfully, and has no mechanism for confirming that what was written into it was ever reviewed by someone with the standing to approve it.

The fourth trigger is the newest and, on first read, the most convincing: a scope chain. When an orchestrator delegates to a sub-agent, the toolkit records the delegation cryptographically, signed, with the capabilities transferred and the restrictions attached, narrowing at every hop. Any agent three or four delegations downstream can trace its authority back through the chain to the human who originally granted it, calling a function built for exactly that purpose. It is a genuinely elegant piece of engineering, and it answers a question Chapter 9 left standing: who is accountable when a chain of agents, not any single one, produces an outcome. The chain can now show its own provenance, cryptographically, end to end.

Read that sentence again, slowly, because the word doing the work is provenance, not authorization. The scope chain proves that a grant of capability traces back, intact and unaltered, to a signature from a named human at the root. It proves the signature is real and the narrowing at each hop was enforced. What it cannot prove is that the root grant itself was ever reviewed against a written scope by someone entitled to accept the risk of what that scope permits. A root sponsor can sign a delegation chain in an afternoon, granting a capability nobody upstream examined, and the cryptography will faithfully certify that afternoon's signature forever. The chain is a perfect record of who clicked, and it is silent on whether anyone should have.

This is the condition Chapter 9 named the Chain Authorization Gap: no authorization record covers what a multi-agent chain collectively did, and no individual agent inside it was ever authorized to do it. A scope chain that proves its own provenance is a better artifact than a chain with no record at all. It is still not an authorization record, because provenance and authorization are answering different questions, the way a notarized signature proves whose hand held the pen and says nothing about whether the person signing had the authority to sign.

## Whose team, whose console

Everything in the last two sections describes a capability. Whether it exists in your tenant is a separate question entirely, and the answer is: only where a specific engineering team decided to adopt it.

The toolkit is open source, MIT licensed, distributed as installable packages across five languages. Nothing about a Microsoft 365 tenant, an Entra directory, or a Copilot Studio environment turns it on. A developer building an agent on Azure AI Foundry has to choose to import it, choose to write the policy file, choose to wire the identity layer into the agent's runtime, and choose to configure the audit backend somewhere durable enough to survive an incident. Where a conscientious team did all four of those things, the toolkit produces exactly the kind of evidence this chapter just credited. Where a different team, on a different agent, in the same tenant, did none of them, there is nothing. Not a weaker version of the audit trail. Nothing. The tenant's coverage is not a policy decision the organization made once. It is the sum of a few hundred individual engineering choices, made or not made, team by team. As of mid-2026, neither the toolkit nor the broader Microsoft stack ships a first-class, tenant-wide inventory of which agents are actually wrapped by it. An organization that wants that view has to build it itself.

This is worth stating without irony, because irony would undersell it: the hash-chained audit log will faithfully and cryptographically prove that a governance decision was tamper-evident, for every agent whose team happened to install the toolkit, and it will prove nothing whatsoever about the agents whose team did not, because those agents generate no chain to inspect in the first place. A tamper-evident record of adoption is not the same thing as evidence of coverage. An examiner asking "which of your three hundred agents run under this governance layer" gets an answer that depends entirely on whether anyone thought to keep a list, and the toolkit does not keep that list for you.

Picture three engineering teams inside the same tenant, building on the same Azure AI Foundry subscription, reporting up through the same CISO. The fraud-detection team, working under a compliance mandate with a named reviewer breathing over their sprint reviews, wired in the full stack: identity, policy, sandboxing, the signed audit chain. Their agent produces the evidence this chapter has been describing. The customer-support team, moving fast under a product deadline, skipped it, because nobody on that team was asked to install it and no gate in the deployment pipeline required it. Their agent runs in the same tenant, reachable through the same Copilot Studio surface, doing work with real customer data, and generating no governance record beyond whatever Purview happens to capture at the platform level. The internal-tools team, somewhere between the two, installed the identity layer for its cleaner engineering ergonomics and never got around to the policy engine, so their agent has a name and a sponsor and nothing enforcing what it can do with either. A registry that lists all three agents as active, healthy, and Copilot Studio-approved is telling the truth and hiding the only fact that matters: three different governance postures, invisible from any console, distinguishable only by asking each team directly what they built. Ask the question an examiner would actually ask, list every agent that touches customer personal data and is governed by this toolkit, and the honest answer today is a spreadsheet someone has to go build, not a report the registry can already run.

That conversation, team by team, is not a scaling strategy. An organization running a few dozen agents can survive on tribal knowledge of who did what. An organization running several hundred cannot, and the toolkit itself supplies no inventory of its own adoption. The gap Chapters 14 and 15 spent their length calling reconciliation is not solved by better tooling at the enforcement layer. It is a separate, organizational obligation the enforcement layer was never built to discharge, and nothing about installing a better kernel changes who has to go find out which agents are running one.

## The exhibit, not the record

Nothing here argues against using the toolkit. An organization running agents on the Microsoft stack that is not evaluating the Agent Governance Toolkit for its production fleet is passing up the best runtime enforcement and evidence-generation engineering currently available on this platform, and this book would say so even if Microsoft had never written a word about the accountability gap itself.

The argument is about where the toolkit's output belongs. A signed delegation chain, a tamper-evident audit log, a require_approval decision with a timestamp and a name attached, all of it belongs inside the authorization record as an exhibit: dated evidence that a specific control fired, for a specific action, at a specific moment. None of it is the authorization record itself, because the authorization record answers a question the toolkit was never built to ask: did a person entitled to accept this risk review this scope, in advance, and sign off on it in a form an examination can accept as current. The toolkit can prove the policy fired. It cannot prove anyone approved the policy.

Picture a police department that equips every officer with a body camera. The footage is excellent. It shows exactly what the officer did, moment by moment, and the recording is tamper-evident enough to survive a defense attorney's scrutiny in court. Nobody who has watched the footage doubts what happened. But the footage cannot show whether the operation itself was authorized, by whom, under what standing order, reviewed by whom in advance. It shows what happened after the camera switched on, at the location where it was issued. It was never pointed at the meeting where someone decided the operation should happen at all.

The Agent Governance Toolkit is the best body camera Microsoft has built for this problem. The tape is good. The tape was never going to answer the question this book keeps asking, because no camera, however well engineered, can point backward into the room where the decision got made, or wasn't.

---

# PART 5: THE RECORD

Everything argued so far compresses into one artifact and one scene. Chapter 18 walks the Agent Authorization Document entry by entry. Chapter 19 brings the examiner back to ask the seven questions of a tenant that kept the record. Chapter 20 is about the forty minutes.

## Chapter 18

# Agent Authorization Document for Microsoft Deployments

One page. Ten entries. No diagrams, no YAML, no hexadecimal beyond a single identifier string. What follows is the least technical artifact in this book, and the one that has been missing from every chapter of it.

The record belongs to an expense-triage agent at a mid-sized company, an agent constructed for this walk rather than reported from any client engagement, built the way Chapter 5 showed thousands of agents get built: by a finance operations manager, in Copilot Studio, in the gaps between her actual job. The agent reads submitted expense reports, compares each one against the published travel policy, drafts a recommendation for the human approver, and routes anything unusual to an exceptions queue.

Unremarkable work. Which is the point. If a record like this exists for the boring agent, the interesting ones have no excuse.

Read it top to bottom, the way an examiner would.

The first entry is the agent's name, and next to the display name, which anyone can change, sits the directory object ID, the hexadecimal string Chapter 12 read off the agent's page in the Microsoft Entra admin center, along with the Blueprint App ID that names its parent blueprint, the template whose posture every agent of its kind inherits. The name answers the question an inventory answers, which one is this, and the identifiers answer it in a form that survives a rename. A record keyed to a display name is keyed to a label someone can edit. A record keyed to the object ID can be joined mechanically to the actor in the logs, which means an examiner holding this page and a Purview export of the agent's activity can connect the decision to what happened without asking anyone to vouch for the match, provided the identity on the page is the identity the agent actually runs under, which is itself a discipline this record exists to enforce.

The second entry is the business purpose, three sentences in the sponsor's own words about the review backlog the agent exists to shrink. This is the entry most likely to be dismissed as redundant, because the agent already has an instructions field and the instructions already describe what it does. Chapter 11 drew the line that matters here: words written to steer a model and words written to commit an organization are different documents even when they overlap, because they face different readers. The instructions field talks to the agent. This paragraph talks to whoever, years from now, has to establish what the organization believed it was deploying.

Then the authorized actions, four of them, each naming a system: read the submissions queue, compare against the policy library, draft a recommendation into the approval workflow, flag exceptions. Then the entry that separates a real record from a form-filling exercise: the explicit prohibitions. This one reads, in full, that the agent may not approve or deny any claim, may not modify any expense record, may not contact any employee directly, and may not touch payroll or personnel data. Notice what kind of writing this is. The actions describe the work, and anyone who watched a demo could draft them. The prohibitions describe the risk somebody sat still long enough to imagine, and they cannot be drafted from the demo, because the demo shows what the agent does, never what it must not do. A blank prohibitions entry is the tell. It does not mean the agent is trusted everywhere. It means the sentence was never finished.

The data access scope names two connectors and one SharePoint library, and visibly resisted the word "etcetera." The business sponsor is a named human, the finance director, one person, with a title, mapped deliberately from the sponsor field the platform populated automatically on the day the agent was created. The technical owner is a named administrator, present so that operations has an address, and marked as what he is not, which is the approving authority. The review triggers list the events that reopen the decision, in the vocabulary Chapter 15 built: scope change, owner departure, regulatory change, incident. The next review date is an actual date, twelve months out, in the future rather than the past.

And at the bottom, the entry the other nine exist to serve: an authorization signature. A name, a title, a date. The signer is the controller, whose written authority already covers the expense process this agent now touches. Not the maker who built it. Not the administrator who registered it. The person entitled to accept what happens if it goes wrong, accepting it, in writing, on a date that precedes the agent's first day of work.

That is the whole document. It fits on one page, an intern could format it, and no platform Microsoft ships generates it today. None ever could, in the only sense that matters: a wizard may someday print the form, but every entry on it is a decision, and the previous seventeen chapters have been one long demonstration that platforms execute decisions and cannot make them. The registry can count this agent. The directory can authenticate it. Purview can log it. The signature is yours.

## Ten entries, ten decisions

Walk the record again, slower, and watch what each entry extracts from the organization, because the form is not documentation. The form is an interrogation.

The identifier entry forces the organization to decide what it is even counting, which Chapter 14 showed is not a clerical question. A record joined to the object ID commits you to a unit of count and an identity model; an agent that exists only as somebody's browser tab cannot be keyed, which surfaces, immediately, the population of things running without registered identities at all. The purpose entry forces a business owner to state, in prose an outsider can evaluate, why this thing should exist, and organizations discover with some regularity that the sentence is harder to write than the agent was to build. The actions and scope entries force the least-privilege conversation every security team claims to want: could the agent still do its stated job with only the access named on this page. If yes, the excess access is a finding the record just produced. If no, the record is wrong and now someone has to fix one or the other, which is the reconciliation between paper and reality that no automated attestation performs.

The prohibitions entry forces someone to imagine failure in advance, on the record, which is the single cheapest form of risk management that exists and the one most reliably skipped. The sponsor and signature entries force the question this book opened with, which named human answers, and force it past the point where a populated directory field can masquerade as the answer. Chapter 2 watched a default write a name into the sponsor attribute and watched everyone downstream read the name as a decision. This record is where the default gets converted or exposed: either the named human accepts the role, in writing, with a date, or the organization discovers that its accountable person was appointed by a click handler.

The triggers and review-date entries force the admission that the decision has a shelf life, which Chapter 15 spent a chapter establishing and one clause can now carry: the approval is a photograph, the agent is a moving subject, and the record must contain its own instructions for when to look again.

There is one more set of names that belongs on this page for any agent whose signals somebody must answer. Chapter 16's protocol requires a person accountable for the agent's accuracy and a person with authority to suspend it, and this record is where those names live, as additional accountability entries, so that the flag, when it fires, routes to a human the paperwork already knows. One document. Every named role in it. Not because consolidation is elegant, but because an examiner asking who answers for this agent should never need a second binder.

Stated plainly, then: the record's entries are not fields. They are the deciding itself, ten organizational judgments this book has spent seventeen chapters proving no platform will render for you, arranged in the order an examination will ask about them, with a place for the one artifact an examination cannot proceed without, a signature from someone entitled to give it. The platform enforces whatever the organization decided. This page is where the deciding leaves evidence.

## Who may sign

Every entry above has an obvious author except the last one, and the last one is where most organizations have no design at all.

Start with what is already settled, because it is worth being precise about which half of this question remains open. Whether the organization answers for its agent's conduct was resolved, outward-facing, by a small-claims tribunal in 2024: Moffatt v. Air Canada established that when the agent speaks, the company has spoken, and no forum since has shown any appetite for the alternative. The unsettled half faces inward. If the organization is bound, which human inside it did the binding, and did anyone with actual authority ever agree to be that human? That question has two possible answering venues. One is a proceeding after the fact, where opposing counsel assembles the answer from consent logs and deposition transcripts, at prices Chapter 2's docket is currently demonstrating. The other is a page like this one, written in advance, by design.

Consider what the tenant currently treats as signing authority. A connector consent dialog appears, an employee clicks accept, and an agent acquires standing access to a system of record. Functionally, that click was a signature. It committed the organization's data, the organization's obligations, and, per the tribunal, the organization's liability, to whatever the agent does next. Now ask who is permitted to click it. The answer, in most tenants, is anyone the license reaches. A tenant can be configured to route the click to an administrator instead, and then the administrator is the one clicking, with the same absent card behind the decision. Your organization caps a manager's wire authority at fifty thousand dollars and reviews the cap annually. The consent dialog ships with no business tier, no monetary limit, and no scheduled review, and it executes a commitment the wire never could: a standing one.

Banking solved this problem before computers existed, and the solution is instructive precisely because it is boring. No bank moves money out of a corporate account on someone's say-so. There is a signature card and a board resolution on file, naming the individuals who may sign, and to what limit, and in what combination for amounts above it. The clerk honoring a signature is not making a judgment about the person; the clerk is checking a document the organization wrote in advance, when nobody was under pressure and nothing was in dispute. Authority was designed, recorded, and bounded before it was ever exercised. Banks keep a signature card for every account. Your tenant keeps none for any agent.

Designing the card for agents is one meeting, not a program. The principle is proportion: the signer for an agent doing given work should hold at least the authority required to assign a human employee the same work. An agent reading one department's documents and drafting summaries signs at the level of the manager who could hire an assistant to do it. An agent writing to systems of record, or speaking to customers in the organization's name, signs at the level of the officer who answers for those records and those customers. An agent that moves money signs wherever human money-movement authority already lives, because the risk did not change genre when the actor stopped being a person. Write the tiers down, and the connector click stops being a signature and becomes what it should have been all along, a technical step inside a process that already produced one.

No new machinery is required. The platform's own governance surfaces, Entra ID Governance access packages among them, already run sponsor-style approvals with expiry for human access, which Chapter 5 conceded, so a signature process has rails to ride on; and none of it is answered by runtime approval gates, which Chapter 17 showed govern whether a configured action executes, not who was entitled to sign the agent into existence. The machinery was never the missing piece. The missing piece is a sentence in a policy saying who may sign, and a page like this one proving they did.

## The half the contract assumes

In the legal department sits the other document people point to when this record is proposed, the vendor agreement, lately grown an AI addendum. It is real paper, heavily negotiated, and Chapter 3 already delivered its verdict in one line: the addendum settles the bill, and the question was about the decision. The verdict deserves one more turn of the screw here, because the addendum does not merely fail to be the authorization record. It quietly depends on one existing.

Read any such contract for what it actually does, and note that nothing in this section is about Microsoft in particular; it is about what contracts are. A contract allocates risk between the two companies whose names are on it. Indemnities, liability caps, acceptable-use commitments, each one a carefully priced answer to the question of which company's insurer is exposed when something goes wrong between them. No internal human appears in it, on either side, because contracts between companies are not in the business of governing the inside of either one. And here is the dependency: nearly every protection the customer negotiated is conditioned, explicitly or practically, on the customer having used the product as intended and approved. The day the organization needs to invoke the contract, it will need to show what its own approved use was. Approved by whom? Scoped how? In writing where? The addendum assumes an internal record it never mentions, and an organization holding a signed contract and no authorization record has paid the premium and cannot file the claim. Two companies signed the external half. Nobody was assigned the internal half, because everybody assumed the external half was the whole document.

**Five artifacts, and the question each one closes**

| The artifact | Governs | Answers | Cannot answer |
|---|---|---|---|
| Enterprise AI policy | The organization | What classes of AI use are permitted here at all | Whether this particular agent was allowed |
| Model or system approval | The capability | Whether the underlying model or platform is fit for use | What this deployment of it may do |
| **Agent Authorization Record** | **The deployment** | **What this agent may do, for whom, on whose signature, until when** | **Whether it was built correctly** |
| Change governance | The modification | Whether a change was reviewed before it shipped | Whether the thing being changed was ever authorized |
| Configuration | The runtime | What the system is currently permitted to reach | Whether anyone decided it should reach it |

*The record sits below policy and above configuration, and it is the only row that names a person. Policy names a class. Approval names a capability. Change governance names an event. Configuration names a permission. The examination question is who decided, and only one of these five rows was built to hold a name.*

## Paper that stays alive

Two properties separate this record from the launch paperwork Chapter 1 watched fail, and both live in how the record is kept rather than what it says.

The first is currency. The review date and the trigger entries are the record's own confession that it will go stale, and the maintenance is exactly the lifecycle Chapter 15 built, pointed at rather than rebuilt: a calendar that forces a look, events that force one sooner, and a re-authorization or a suspension at the end of the look, those being the available verbs. A record reviewed and re-signed carries its history forward; the prior version goes to the archive, not the shredder, because the sequence of decisions is itself evidence of a functioning process.

The second property is harder and almost nobody designs for it. The record's entire value is that it predates whatever event makes someone want to read it, and predating has to be provable by something other than the date typed at the top of the page. A record living in an editable document on someone's desktop satisfies all ten entries and fails the only test an adversarial reader will run, which is whether this paper could have been produced last night. Keep the record where creation is timestamped and versions are preserved beyond the author's reach, a repository with retention holds, a system whose history cannot be quietly rewritten, so that the question of when the decision was made is answered by infrastructure rather than by the sincerity of the person who wrote it down. For institutions under the banking agencies' model risk guidance, which excluded agentic AI from its scope in April 2026 while directing firms to cover the gap through their own governance practices, no supervisory letter names this record; what the guidance expects is that scope, approvals, and limits be documented and reviewable, this page concentrates that expectation for a single agent, and a prudential examiner's first question about any artifact is when it came into existence.

Which surfaces the last uncomfortable case, the common one: the agent that is already running, has been for two years, and has no record at all. Writing this page for it now is the right move and a trap at the same time, and the difference is a label. The verbs available are the ones Chapter 14 fixed: authorize it now, with today's date and a scope someone reviewed today, or suspend it until someone will. What today's signature cannot do is reach backward. A memo explaining the last two years can exist, filed under its own honest name, but this record is not that memo. Its signature commits the organization from its date forward, and the agent's Created On field in the directory will keep saying what it says. The two dates will not match. They are not supposed to match. They are both supposed to be true, and the distance between them is a fact about your governance that the record preserves instead of papering over, which is the difference between a document an examiner trusts and a document an examiner tests.

The organization that sits down to complete this page for a running agent tends to expect a filing exercise and gets an excavation instead. The purpose has three candidate authors and no agreed sentence. The prohibitions have never been imagined by anyone in daylight. The sponsor learns, in the meeting, that she is the sponsor. The signature line waits on a question about signing authority that turns out never to have been asked in the agent's lifetime, or the tenant's. None of those discoveries was caused by the form. Every one of them was sitting in production the whole time, unwritten, which is the only place a decision can hide.

**Signature authority, and what makes each one hold**

| The signer | What their signature establishes | When it fails to hold |
|---|---|---|
| The technical owner | The agent does what the record describes | Signed alone. Technical accuracy is not risk acceptance. |
| The business sponsor | The purpose is legitimate and the risk is accepted | Signed by someone without authority to accept that magnitude of risk |
| The approving authority | The organization has decided this may operate | Signed after deployment, which makes it ratification, not authorization |
| All three, dated | The decision existed before the action | The date is missing, in which case none of the above holds |

*A record that cannot prove its own date is not evidence. A record signed only by the person who built the agent is a description, not an authorization.*

# Chapter 19

# The Examiner Returns

The conference room is the same. The projector is newer.

Eighteen months have passed since the morning Chapter 1 watched from the doorway, the morning an advisory landed and a general counsel asked who approved Copilot reading labeled mail and the room produced silence, then archaeology. The organization in that room is the one this chapter returns to, moved forward a year and a half and given the particulars a scene requires. What follows is a constructed examination scenario, built to match documented regulatory patterns rather than drawn from any specific real examination, and the organization is constructed with it: a mid-sized financial services company, Microsoft stack throughout, agents in production across Copilot, Copilot Studio, Power Platform, and two custom builds on Microsoft Foundry. Everything it produces in this chapter was built in the preceding eighteen chapters. Nothing in the folder is new. That is the point of the folder.

The examiner is the same too, and she has done what examiners do. The document request arrived three weeks in advance, and its first line is the request Chapter 1 predicted: produce the authorization record, the named owner, and the last review evidence for the five most active agents in the last quarter. The list around that line is longer than it was eighteen months ago; the supervisory attention Chapter 1 began citing has kept hardening from principle into procedure, and document requests harden with it. The meeting that follows is not a discussion. It is a production, and the difference between this meeting and the one eighteen months ago is that when the first question is asked, somebody opens a folder instead of a search bar.

She asks her seven questions in the order she always asks them, population first, then the single record, then the compositions, then the question of whether any of it is still true. The questions have not changed. Examination questions do not change; that is what makes them examination questions. What has changed is the other side of the table.

## The production

### How many AI agents are operating in your environment right now, and how does that number compare to the number your organization approved?

The platform's half of this answer arrives on one screen: the registry's summary tiles report what the directory can see, a running count, the unowned, the unmanaged. The organization's half arrives as a report with a cover page, the quarterly reconciliation, and the report is where the question actually gets answered, because the two numbers the examiner asked for are both in it. Under the company's written counting rule, two hundred eighty-nine agents are operating: the registry's two hundred forty-seven, plus the populations the directory reads as something else and the rule refuses to, the Copilot Studio builds that predate the July 2026 identity cutover, the Power Automate flows that call a model and act on the result, and two vendor services with tenant data access that no console lists. The rule counts what acts on model output because that is the question the examiner asked. The flows that act without a model sit in the same register under their own heading, on Chapter 6's reasoning that determinism describes how a system decides and not what its decisions touch. Against the two hundred eighty-nine stands the register of approvals: two hundred sixty-two agents with a standing authorization, a named owner, and a review date. The remaining twenty-seven are in the report too, by name, each with a tier, a discovery date, and a disposition deadline, because the reconciliation that found them is the same control that reports them.

The examiner writes down three numbers, and none of them surprises her, because the organization handed her all three before she could ask. The count is not clean. It is reconciled, which is a different and more useful property. A clean count is a claim. A reconciled count is a procedure, and the procedure is what she is examining.

**For this agent: who authorized it, and what exactly was it authorized to do?**

For each of the five sampled agents the platform's half is the sponsor field, a named human the directory has maintained since creation. The organization's half is the page behind the field. The most active of the five is a payment-exceptions triage agent, and its authorization record reads the way Chapter 18 read one: identifiers keyed to the directory object, a business purpose in the sponsor's own words, four authorized actions, a prohibitions entry that somebody visibly finished writing, a data scope that names its connectors, and, at the bottom, a signature. A name, a title, a date, and the date precedes the agent's first day in production by eleven days. The examiner checks exactly that arithmetic, because it is the arithmetic that separates an authorization from an explanation.

**When it acts outside that scope, which named human answers? Not a team. A name.**

The directory's schema can hold the name; that was never the gap. The gap was the follow-up, show me where they agreed, and the follow-up is answered by handing her the place where they agreed. The signature block on the record is one person, the operations controller, whose written signing authority under the company's delegation matrix covers the payment process the agent touches. She did not inherit the role from a default. The record shows the sponsor field's machine-populated name being deliberately confirmed, in writing, by a person who understood what confirming meant. Eighteen months ago the same question would have produced a populated attribute and a hopeful inference. Today it produces a page, and the page produces a person, and the person, interviewed later that week, describes the agent's scope from memory and gets it right.

**This outcome came from multiple agents acting in sequence. Whose authorization covers the chain?**

One of the five samples is a composition: the exceptions agent hands cases to a customer-notification agent, two authorized systems one dropdown apart, exactly the shape Chapter 9 assembled. The platform's half is what it has always been, identity lineage and per-service logs, handoffs timestamped where the service supports it. The organization's half is a record no platform generates: a chain authorization, one page, naming both agents by identifier, describing the aggregate of what the pair can do that neither was individually approved to do, and signed by an officer whose authority covers the composed outcome, dated before the connection was made rather than after it was discovered. The record exists because somebody read the change ticket and recognized that connecting two authorized agents is a third authorization event, which is the entire lesson of the Chain Authorization Gap applied one Tuesday at a time. The examiner reads the page twice. Chain records are still rare enough to read twice.

**Your systems of record show the change the agent made. Can they show who sanctioned it?**

The platform's half is complete and always was: the audit trail, the application logs, the agent's own identity on the entries it wrote. The organization's half is the join. The examiner picks one change the exceptions agent made in May, a case routed and a record annotated, and the production team lays two documents side by side: the log export showing the change under the agent's directory identity, and the authorization record keyed to that same object ID, its authorized-actions entry covering exactly that class of change. The log supplied the change and the page supplied the sanction, joined mechanically by an identifier rather than testimonially by whoever happens to be in the room. Chapter 13 walked the substrate that makes the first document possible and priced it. This meeting is where the second document earns its keep, because without it, the first document answers, at length, a question nobody asked.

**Your monitoring flagged this before the incident. What were you required to do when the flag fired, and did you do it?**

The platform supplied the flag; it always does. In April, a data-security alert fired on the notification agent, sensitive content touched in a pattern the policy watched for, an alert of the kind Chapter 13 priced. Eighteen months ago that alert would have been an opportunity, closed as informational by an analyst answering the question the console asked. What the examiner is handed instead is a small stack: the alert itself, the protocol page from the agent's record naming the person required to receive it, by name and by role, the threshold that made this alert a trigger rather than noise, and a decision memo dated four days later, inside the ten-business-day window the record specifies, documenting a hold, the review that followed, and the resumption under an amended scope. Required is the word the examiner's question turns on, and the stack answers it in the only grammar examinations accept. The organization was told, the organization was obligated, and the organization can prove the obligation was met, with dates.

**Is any of this current? When was this authorization last revisited, and what change would have forced a revisit?**

The Microsoft column of this answer is blank, and Chapter 3 already said why the blank is honest: the stack never held the acceptance, so it has nothing to refresh. The organizational column is the thickest part of the folder. Each sampled record carries its last review date, the decision the review produced, and the archived prior version underneath it, because a stack of dated decisions is its own species of evidence, proof that the process runs and not merely that it exists. The triggers are listed and have visibly fired: one agent was re-authorized early when its scope changed, another when its owner resigned, and the register is careful about what did not count as a review. The company runs access reviews in Entra and on its SharePoint sites like everyone else, and its record states plainly what those recertify, who holds access and who belongs to a site, and what they do not, which is whether anyone still stands behind the agent's acceptance; the acceptance gets its own recertification, and the register is where that one is scheduled, and nothing else is allowed to impersonate it. When an owner departs, the platform's orphaned-object menu reassigns the ownership, and the register adds the step the menu has never carried, a re-authorization by the incoming owner or a suspension until someone signs. Drift is watched the same way: the coverage ratio is recomputed quarterly, and movement in it is treated as an early finding rather than a curiosity. And one line in the register records the other kind of currency, an agent retired last autumn by a documented governance decision, the third ending Chapter 7 watched a city reach by budget line instead.

Taken together, the decisions behind these seven answers are what the framework library collects under the name Organizational Agent Controls: the small set of decisions only the deploying organization can make, about identity, scope, ownership, monitoring obligations, and endings, with the platform enforcing whichever ones the organization actually made. Nothing in the name is new to this room. The company has been making the decisions for eighteen months. The name is just where the decisions live when someone asks for them as a set.

The examination Chapter 1 staged has now been answered in full, and the shape of every answer was the same shape seven times. The platform's contribution arrived in one clause, real and conceded. The rest was paper the organization wrote, signed, and kept current, produced on request, joined to the telemetry by identifiers instead of by memory. Eighteen months ago the sentence at the center of this book described a gap. In this room it describes a division of labor.

*The platform proved what the agent did. You proved what it was allowed to do.*

## Four interviews, four documents

Chapter 2 ran four interviews at an insurer and got four confident answers pointing at four other chairs. The examiner runs the same four interviews here, in the same order, because examiners run them too.

The builder, a finance operations analyst who assembled a reporting agent in Copilot Studio last spring, is asked who approved it. She does not say the license was the approval. She produces the intake ticket, because since the reconciliation installed its gate, agents enter production through intake or not at all, and the gate was built so that using it costs less than avoiding it. Her ticket took her twenty minutes and came back in four days with a tier, a named sponsor, and a record number.

The platform administrator is asked what he reviews. His answer is unchanged, capacity, policy boundaries, tenant hygiene, and he is no longer embarrassed by it, because he can produce the page that says whose job the use-case review actually is. His domain stops where the register begins, in writing.

The business owner, a vice president whose team runs three of the sampled agents, is asked what stands behind them. Her old belief, that anything on the corporate platform passed security review, has been replaced by something less comfortable and more durable: her signature, on three records, with three review dates she can recite because two of them are next quarter.

Security is asked when they first heard of the reporting agent. The answer is a date, from the intake queue, before it ran. First is no longer a synonym for too late.

Four people, four documents, and the circle Chapter 2 traced has been cut in the only way circles get cut. Nobody points at another chair, because the question now has an address. The interviews still take an afternoon. They are just no longer the discovery phase.

## The finding

None of this reads as a victory lap to the examiner, because examinations do not end in laps. They end in findings, and she writes one.

The fourth sampled agent, a collections-outreach assistant, shows an annual review completed nineteen days after its due date. The record does not hide the gap; the review is dated, the delay is visible, and the interview establishes the reason, which is that the reviewing officer was on leave in August and the review waited for her return. The examiner then asks the question the delay exists to provoke. What does the register say happens when the reviewer is unavailable? The register says nothing. Eighteen months of genuinely good design, and nobody wrote the alternate-reviewer provision, the clause the company's own delegation of authority matrix has carried for decades, the provision Chapter 1 noticed in passing for an approver who is away. The finance discipline solved reviewer absence before anyone in the room was born. The agent register, young and proud of itself, met its first August unprepared.

The finding is written formally: review-cadence control operated outside its defined timeline for one in-scope system; the control lacks a continuity provision; management response due in thirty days. The response, drafted the following week, is one paragraph amending the register's procedure and one calendar rule. The examiner also records, as an observation rather than a finding, the twenty-seven unregistered agents from the reconciliation report, noting that the population was self-identified, tiered, and dated by the organization's own control before the examination began, with dispositions in flight under the only two verbs the register permits, authorize now or suspend.

Weigh what just happened, because it is the honest version of the ending this book has been promising. The prepared organization did not escape the examination clean. It took a finding, in exactly the place mature disciplines take findings, at the seam where a young process has not yet copied an old process's scar tissue. What it escaped was the other meeting: the archaeology, the deployment ticket offered as a risk decision, the four-month remediation program staffed by everyone who once said someone else was tracking this. Its finding cost a paragraph. The alternative costs a war room, and the difference between the two was not purchased from any vendor. It was written, one page at a time, by people who decided the questions were coming.

They are coming. The organization in this chapter is constructed. The examiner is not; she publishes her observations, she trains her colleagues, and her request list has been public since Chapter 1 quoted it. Somewhere in your own tenant tonight, the five most active agents of the quarter are finishing their shift, and the folder that would answer for them either exists or it does not. The meeting has two versions. You have read both now. The only detail still undecided is which one your organization is currently rehearsing, and it is deciding that detail today, in the quietest possible way, by writing the records or not writing them, while nobody is asking yet.

---

### Four interviews, four documents

| The party | What the examiner asks | What they produce now |
|---|---|---|
| The builder | Who approved it | An intake ticket carrying a tier, a sponsor, and a number |
| The platform administrator | What he reviews | The page assigning use-case review to someone else |
| The business owner | What stands behind these agents | Three signatures and three review dates |
| Security | When they first heard of it | A queue entry predating the agent |

*The same four chairs as Chapter 2, the same four questions, and four documents instead of four gestures. What changed is not the confidence. It is that the confidence is now attached to paper somebody signed.*

## Chapter 20

# Forty Minutes That Prevent Four Months

The document gets written on a Thursday, at a desk, between a 3:00 meeting that ran long and a 4:15 that will start on time.

The writer is an accounts-payable manager at a distribution company, constructed for this scene the way this book's organizations have been constructed throughout, and the agent is hers. She built it in Copilot Studio in March, on her own initiative, without a project code, which is how most of the agents in this book got built. It matches supplier invoices to purchase orders and routes mismatches to a human queue. It has been running for eleven weeks. Nothing about this afternoon was triggered by an incident, an advisory, or an examiner. Her company adopted an intake rule a month ago, every agent gets an authorization record or gets suspended, and her agent's deadline is Friday.

She opens the template and starts the clock.

The identifiers take two minutes, because they are copied, not composed. The Microsoft Entra admin center supplies the object ID off the agent's own page, the string that survives a rename, and the display name goes next to it, demoted to a label. Two minutes, most of it navigation.

The purpose takes eight. Three sentences, in her own words, about the mismatch backlog the agent exists to shrink, who relied on the old manual process, and what the queue receives now instead. She resists the urge to paste the agent's instructions here, because the instructions were written to steer a model and this paragraph is written to commit a company, and the two audiences do not read the same way. The sentences come slowly because they are for a reader she will never meet, some future person holding this page and asking what the organization believed it was deploying. Eight minutes to say it plainly is not slow. It is the fastest anyone will ever answer that question again.

The authorized actions take five. Four lines, written from memory, because she built the thing: read invoices from the AP mailbox, read purchase orders from the finance system, write match results to the exceptions list, notify the queue. Memory is sufficient here. Everything in this entry was decided months ago; the writing is transcription.

The data reach takes four minutes, written as the named connectors rather than as a category of information, because a connector can be checked and a category can only be debated.

Then the prohibitions, and the clock slows down, because nothing in this entry was ever decided at all. Nobody has asked her what the agent must never do, including her. The first two lines come easily: it never approves an invoice, it never releases a payment. The third one stops her. Should it ever contact a supplier? It cannot today. It could after one connector and one enthusiastic quarter, a shared mailbox pointed at supplier addresses instead of an internal queue, and the page is asking about authority, not current wiring. She sits with it, decides no, and writes the sentence: it never communicates outside the company. Twelve minutes, most of them spent deciding rather than typing, which is the correct ratio. The prohibitions are the only entry on the page that requires the organization to make up its mind, and the blank space where they should be is what the deferral was protecting.

The owner entry takes three minutes and one hallway. Her own name goes in as owner, because the page wants a person who can describe the agent's scope without looking it up, and that person is objectively her. The sponsor line above it needs her director, so she walks the forty feet, explains the page, and watches him slow down at the prohibitions before he nods. His signature waits for Tuesday, when the operations meeting can put it next to the delegation matrix that says he may give it. The signing waits. The writing did not have to.

The review date takes two minutes: twelve months out, plus a calendar rule that fires the review to whoever holds the owner entry at the time, not to her by name, because owners change.

Total the clock and it comes to roughly forty minutes, and the number should be handled honestly, because this book has spent nineteen chapters demanding sourced claims and is not going to end by inventing a statistic. Forty minutes is an estimate of a writing act, made about a constructed afternoon, generous in both directions. Under an hour on a slow day, over it if the prohibitions surface a real dispute, and if they do, the dispute is the deliverable. Nothing in the argument rides on the stopwatch. What rides on the afternoon is the date at the bottom of the page, which now precedes whatever happens next.

## The other version of the page

The same page gets written a second way, and the second way also has a clock.

That version is drafted in a conference room booked through the end of the quarter, in month two of a remediation program, after the finding. The room holds two contractors, a program manager, a rotating chair from the affected business line, and an associate general counsel on Thursdays. The wall holds a tracker. The tracker holds one line per agent, and each line ends in the same deliverable: the page from this chapter's first section, reconstructed at distance.

Reconstruction is the operative word. The purpose paragraph is drafted by a contractor interviewing a builder, where the builder is still employed; the invoice-matching agent's counterpart here was built by someone who left in June, so its purpose is being assembled from a demo recording and a hopeful reading of the instructions field. The authorized actions are recovered from run logs, which document what the agent has done, a different list from what it was permitted to do, related but not interchangeable. The prohibitions are the worst of it. The room can establish what the agent has been observed not to do. Observed restraint is not a prohibition; it is an absence with good manners, and everyone at the table knows the difference, which is why this entry takes the longest in this room too. The prohibitions are the long entry in both rooms. The difference is who is deciding them, and the people deciding them here never met the agent.

And then there are the dates. A record written in month two of a remediation can be made accurate about everything except the one thing an examiner checks first, which is when the deciding happened. The page in the first room says the decision preceded the operation. The page in this room can only say the decision has now, at last, been written down, and it must say so out loud, because Chapter 18's label rule holds: a reconstructed record that pretends to be an original one is not late paperwork, it is a false statement with a signature on it. The war room produces the same page at a blended contractor rate.

Call this version four months. That number is also an estimate, drawn from the shape these programs take once a finding starts the clock and counsel joins the standing meeting, and it is also generous. Nothing rides on that stopwatch either. What rides on it is everything else the four months carry: the burn rate, the pulled staff, the business line answering interview requests instead of running, and a regulator reading each reconstructed page while holding, in the other hand, the log of when it was created.

Forty minutes of writing, or four months of remediation. It is the same document either way.

## Why it was never written

Every explanation an organization reaches for first turns out to be wrong. Eliminate them in order; the one left standing is the reason the page does not exist.

Not cost. The page requires no license, no procurement, no vendor, and no software beyond a template and a directory lookup. It may be the only artifact in enterprise AI with no line item at all, which turns out to be part of the problem: work that cheap never gets a project code, and work without a project code never gets assigned.

Not tooling. The directory already holds the identifiers. The run histories and the audit logs already hold the activity. Chapters 4 through 17 walked an entire platform's worth of machinery, and none of it was the missing piece, because the missing piece is a page of organizational English that no console can emit. The tooling objection dies on a simple observation: the first room in this chapter contained a template, a browser tab, and a person. The company had all three the whole time.

Not knowledge, either, or at least not mostly. Watch where the forty minutes actually went. The identifiers were copied. The purpose and the actions were transcribed from a memory that already held them. Nearly everything on the page was already known by somebody; it was just never committed anywhere a second person could find it. The exception is the prohibitions, the twelve minutes of genuine deciding, and that exception explains more than it seems to. Writing the page forces the one decision the organization had been deferring, and an unwritten page keeps the deferral invisible. The blank record was never an oversight sitting in a queue. It was a decision not yet made, wearing an oversight's clothes.

Which leaves the real reason, and it is the one this book opened with. Nobody was assigned to write the page, and everybody assumed someone had, the same assumption Chapter 2 watched four people make about each other in a conference room. The record went unwritten for exactly the reason the agent went unowned. Closing the loop costs one sentence in one policy, the sentence the accounts-payable manager's company finally wrote: every agent gets a record, signed by its owner, or gets suspended. The sentence is cheap, and what it does is convert the page from an opportunity into an obligation, a distance Chapter 16 already priced by the minute.

A reader running a real tenant has been doing multiplication for two paragraphs now, so do it openly. Three hundred agents at forty minutes each is two hundred hours, which is five weeks of one person's life and an obvious non-starter. It is also the wrong arithmetic. The page is written by the owner, because the owner is the person who can write it from memory, which means the real cost is forty minutes per owner, distributed across the population that built the agents in the first place. The multiplication only fails for the agents whose owner cannot be found to spend the forty minutes, and for those, the failed multiplication is the finding, delivered early and free of charge. An agent that cannot claim forty minutes of anyone's attention is an agent nobody owns, and it is considerably cheaper to learn that from a template than from a request list.

## The number

One question remains, and it is not one of the examiner's seven. Those were hers. This one is yours.

Of the agents operating in your environment right now, how many have this page?

Notice what reaching for the answer does. It requires two numbers, a count of agents and a count of records, and the first number has to come from somewhere more honest than the last slide deck that quoted one. If the first number is not available, the question was answered before it finished being asked. The count you cannot produce is the answer.

The page is not optional. Only its date is. Some version of it will be written for every agent that matters, by an owner at a desk or by contractors in month two, dated before the questions or after them, and the choice between those versions is almost never made deliberately. It is made by assignment or by its absence, which means your organization is making it now, in whichever direction its silence points. The document costs forty minutes. Assigning it costs a sentence. The four months are the price of the sentence nobody wrote.

---

**The same agent, two versions of its file**

| | The version that took forty minutes | The version that takes four months |
|---|---|---|
| When it was written | Before anyone asks, while the people who decided are still there | After the request list arrives |
| Who wrote it | The people who knew the answers | People reconstructing what others decided |
| What it costs to produce | One meeting | Legal hours, examination response, remediation program |
| What it proves | The decision existed | That the organization can assemble a narrative |
| What the examiner concludes | The control was designed | The control was reverse-engineered from the finding |

*The forty minutes are not cheaper because the work is smaller. They are cheaper because the people who could answer are still in the building, and because the answer has not yet become a position the organization must defend.*

# APPENDIX A: THE AGENT AUTHORIZATION RECORD

Complete one record per deployed agent. Retain it as a governance artifact, in storage that can prove the record's date. Chapter 18 walks a completed example; this page is the blank.

AGENT NAME The display name used in the agent registry, admin center, or internal inventory, keyed where possible to a stable platform identifier.

BUSINESS PURPOSE One to three sentences: the problem this agent solves and the workflow it supports.

AUTHORIZED ACTIONS Each action the agent is permitted to take, in precise language tied to specific systems or workflows.

EXPLICIT PROHIBITIONS What the agent must not do. A blank here means the record is incomplete.

DATA ACCESS SCOPE The systems, libraries, sites, datasets, and applications the agent can read from and write to.

BUSINESS SPONSOR Full name and title of the one named human accountable for the business authorization decision. Where the platform's sponsor role holds a group, this record still names one person.

TECHNICAL OWNER Full name and title of the administrator responsible for operational management, permissions, and identity configuration. Not the approving authority. Where a monitoring obligation attaches, name here who answers for the agent's accuracy and who can suspend it in production (Chapter 16).

REVIEW TRIGGER CONDITIONS The events that require re-authorization: a change in purpose, data access, ownership, or regulation, or an incident.

NEXT SCHEDULED REVIEW DATE The date the organization will confirm this record is still accurate and complete.

AUTHORIZATION SIGNATURE The approving person's name, title, and date. The accountable business owner, not only the developer or administrator.

# Appendix A: The Agent Authorization Record

This template is a base. Adapt it into your organization's own governance forms rather than adopting it verbatim.
Adapted from Sougata Roy, "Agent Authorization Document," sougataroy.com/frameworks/agent-authorization-document (first published April 2026); also deposited in The Authorization Layer framework library, Zenodo, July 2026, DOI 10.5281/zenodo.21245690, licensed CC BY 4.0.

---

**The ten fields, and what each survives**

| The field answers | The examination question it closes | What it is worth if undated |
|---|---|---|
| Name, purpose, permitted actions | What was this for? | Nothing. An undated purpose describes an intention, not an authorization. |
| Prohibitions, data scope | What was it not allowed to do? | Nothing. The prohibition must predate the act. |
| Sponsor, technical owner | Who answers for it? | Nothing. An owner named after the incident is a respondent, not an owner. |
| Review triggers, next review date | When does this get re-examined? | Nothing. A review that was never scheduled was never required. |
| Signature and date | Who allowed this, and when? | Everything else on the page depends on this line. |

*A record that cannot prove its own date is not evidence.*

# APPENDIX B: FIFTY QUESTIONS

These are not a checklist. A checklist implies that ticking every box produces a governed agent, and it does not. These are the questions an examiner, a plaintiff's counsel, or a board member will ask, arranged by the moment in an agent's life when someone still has time to answer them cheaply.

Take the stage that matches where your agent is now. Ask the questions out loud, in the room, with the people who would have to answer them under oath. If the answers come slowly, that is the finding. If the answers come quickly and nobody can produce the document behind them, that is a different finding, and a worse one.

Each question names the framework it comes from, and where a framework has named parts, the part rather than its position in a list. The frameworks are described in the chapters; the questions are what the frameworks sound like when someone is asking you.

---

## STAGE ONE: BEFORE AUTHORIZATION

*Every question in the five stages that follow is either answered cheaply here or made expensive later.*

**1.** Who is the single named person who will explain this agent to an examiner in three years, and have they accepted that accountability in writing? *(The Accountability Assumption)*

**2.** What is this agent explicitly prohibited from doing, and where is that written in a form that survives the departure of everyone in this room? *(Agent Authorization Record)*

**3.** What data can this agent reach that its stated purpose does not require, and who decided that access was acceptable anyway? *(Intent Architecture)*

**4.** What is the specific number at which this agent's performance stops being a concern and becomes a formal review, and who chose that number? *(Disposition Protocol, the trigger threshold)*

**5.** Which named person can pause this agent in production without convening a meeting, and has anyone tested that they can? *(Disposition Protocol, the suspension authority)*

**6.** If this agent is approved today and nobody ever reviews it, on what date does its authorization expire? *(Authorization Coverage Lifecycle)*

**7.** Before this agent resumes after any suspension, what specifically must be demonstrated, and was that standard written before deployment or will it be written while the business is waiting? *(Disposition Protocol, the re-authorization standard)*

**8.** Who has a right to know if this agent fails, and how many hours do they get to wait before being told? *(Disposition Protocol, the notification clock)*

**9.** Is the person authorizing this agent the same person who wants it deployed, and if so, what makes this an authorization rather than a formality? *(The Accountability Assumption)*

---

## STAGE TWO: AT DEPLOYMENT

*The stage where the authorization record either becomes true or becomes a document about a different system.*

**10.** Does the agent that shipped do what the agent that was authorized was described as doing, and who compared the two? *(The Intent Gap)*

**11.** Whose credentials does this agent run on, and if it is a person's, what happens to the agent when that person changes roles or leaves the organization? *(Organizational Agent Controls)*

**12.** Which parts of this agent's behavior does the platform vendor guarantee, which parts does your control infrastructure guarantee, and which parts does nobody guarantee? *(Deployment Accountability Map)*

**13.** If this agent can be triggered by an event rather than a person, who reviewed the events, and is the list of permitted triggers closed? *(Organizational Agent Controls)*

**14.** What can this agent do that no human in the approval chain has ever watched it do? *(Agent Substrate Readiness Model)*

**15.** Is this agent registered anywhere that an examiner could find it, or only in the system where it was built? *(Tenant Agent Reconciliation)*

**16.** If this agent were deployed today by a team that never spoke to governance, what in your environment would stop it? *(Authorization Coverage Lifecycle)*

**17.** Does the logging on this agent capture what it was permitted to do, or only what it did? *(Intent Architecture)*

---

## STAGE THREE: IN OPERATION

*The stage that lasts the longest and gets reviewed the least.*

**18.** When this agent calls another agent, which authorization covers the second one, and which covers the delegation itself? *(Chain Authorization Gap)*

**19.** How many agents are currently operating in your tenant, and how confident are you in that number to the nearest ten? *(Tenant Agent Reconciliation)*

**20.** Which of your agents have no named owner, and how long have they been running that way? *(Shadow Agent Inventory)*

**21.** When did this agent's scope last change, who approved the change, and was the authorization record updated on the same day? *(Authorization Coverage Lifecycle)*

**22.** If a chain of four agents produces an outcome nobody would have approved, which of the four was operating outside its scope? *(Chain Authorization Gap)*

**23.** What is this agent doing at three in the morning, and who reads that? *(Organizational Agent Controls)*

**24.** Can you produce, today, the list of every system this agent has touched in the last ninety days? *(Intent Architecture)*

**25.** If an agent in your environment began behaving outside its intent tomorrow, how would you learn about it, and from whom? *(Disposition Protocol, the accuracy owner)*

**26.** Which agents in your tenant were built by someone who has since left the organization? *(Shadow Agent Inventory)*

**27.** Does anyone review what your agents are permitted to do, or only what they have done? *(The Intent Gap)*

---

## STAGE FOUR: AT REVIEW

*The stage most organizations schedule and then move.*

**28.** What percentage of your deployed agents have a complete authorization record, and when did you last calculate it rather than estimate it? *(Authorization Coverage Lifecycle)*

**29.** Is that percentage going up or down, and would you know within a quarter if it reversed? *(Authorization Coverage Lifecycle)*

**30.** Can the executive accountable for AI governance report the current coverage ratio to the board without assembling the data first? *(Authorization Coverage Lifecycle)*

**31.** When a new agent is proposed in your organization, is the first question how to complete governance intake or how to get around it? *(Governance Readiness Matrix)*

**32.** Which agents were reviewed this cycle because the calendar said so, and which were reviewed because something changed? *(Disposition Protocol)*

**33.** How many of your agents' business sponsors could describe, unprompted, what the agent they sponsor actually does? *(The Accountability Assumption)*

**34.** Does your agent count from IT match your agent count from the business units, and if not, which number appears in the board materials? *(Tenant Agent Reconciliation)*

**35.** Is your audit trail adequate for the specific regulatory framework you operate under, and who tested that claim rather than merely asserting it? *(Authorization Coverage Lifecycle)*

**36.** What did last cycle's review find, and what changed as a result? *(Governance Readiness Matrix)*

---

## STAGE FIVE: ON DRIFT OR INCIDENT

*The stage where the documents written months ago are either evidence or embarrassment.*

**37.** The threshold was crossed on a Friday afternoon. Who received the signal, and what were they formally obligated to do next? *(Disposition Protocol, the accuracy owner)*

**38.** Every metric looked fine and the outcome was still wrong. Who is permitted to raise that, and does raising it start the same clock a threshold crossing would? *(Disposition Protocol, the trigger threshold)*

**39.** Who paused it, and did they need permission to do so? *(Disposition Protocol, the suspension authority)*

**40.** When one agent in a running chain is paused, what happens to the downstream agents that still hold its last handoff? *(Chain Authorization Gap)*

**41.** Can the agent be suspended without calling the original developer or going back into the original development environment? *(Disposition Protocol, the suspension authority)*

**42.** A decision is required within the defined window. What is the default if the window closes without one? *(Disposition Protocol, the decision window)*

**43.** Was the notification sent because a clock required it, or because someone eventually decided it was time? *(Disposition Protocol, the notification clock)*

**44.** When this is over, will the record show only what the agent did, or will it also show who allowed it? *(The Accountability Assumption)*

---

## STAGE SIX: AT RETIREMENT

*The stage almost nobody designs, and the one that leaves credentials alive in production.*

**45.** When this agent is decommissioned, what happens to the credentials it was running on? *(Organizational Agent Controls)*

**46.** Who confirms that a retired agent has actually stopped executing, instead of merely being marked inactive? *(Tenant Agent Reconciliation)*

**47.** What happens to the records this agent produced, and for how long is someone required to keep them? *(Intent Architecture)*

**48.** If the agent is retired and its business sponsor has left, who signs the closure? *(The Accountability Assumption)*

**49.** Which agents in your environment are still authorized but no longer used, and how do they differ from the ones you would call shadow agents? *(Shadow Agent Inventory)*

**50.** Six months from now, could you prove this agent was retired on the exact date you say it was? *(Agent Authorization Record)*

*Fifty questions. If your organization can answer all fifty with documents rather than recollection, the authorization architecture described in this book is already built. If it cannot, the gap between the two is not a technology problem, and no platform release will close it.*

*This appendix may be reproduced for internal governance use with attribution to Sougata Roy, Who Owns the Agent? Enterprise AI Accountability on the Microsoft Stack, 2026. The current version is maintained at sougataroy.com/who-owns-the-agent-annex.*

# APPENDIX C: REFERENCE TABLES

# Appendix C: Reference Tables

Framework | Chapter | The question it answers

## Frameworks, chapters, and the question each answers

| Framework | Chapter | The question it answers |
|---|---|---|
| The Accountability Assumption | 2 | Why does everyone believe someone else governed this? |
| Deployment Accountability Map | 7 | Where does the vendor's responsibility end and mine begin? |
| The Chain Authorization Gap | 9 | Who authorized what the chain did together? |
| The Authorization Layer | 10 | What sits beneath the controls that are all reporting green? |
| Intent Architecture | 11 | What was this agent supposed to do, and who said so? |
| Agent Substrate Readiness Model | 13 | What can the platform prove, and what drifts underneath it? |
| Tenant Agent Reconciliation | 14 | What is actually running here? |
| Governance Readiness Matrix | 14 | Where does this organization actually sit? |
| Authorization Coverage Lifecycle | 15 | Is the gap growing or closing? |
| The Disposition Protocol | 16 | What happens when it goes wrong, and who decides? |
| Organizational Agent Controls | 19 | What does an examiner need to see? |
| The Agent Authorization Record | 18, Appendix A | What does the document itself contain? |

## Every role the book requires a name for

| The role | Named when | What they own | What happens if unnamed |
|---|---|---|---|
| Business sponsor | Before deployment | Purpose and risk acceptance | The agent operates on borrowed authority |
| Technical owner | Before deployment | Configuration and scope accuracy | Nobody can say what the agent actually reaches |
| Accuracy owner | Before deployment | Receiving every signal and deciding what follows | Alerts arrive somewhere and stop |
| Suspension authority | Before deployment, distinct from the accuracy owner | Pausing production while a review runs | Stopping requires a meeting, during an incident |
| Approving authority | Before deployment | The organization's decision that this may operate | Deployment proceeded without a decision |
| Consequence owner | Before deployment | Answering for the agent's behavior | The examiner's third question has no answer |

*Six roles. In most deployments they collapse into one person, who is usually the person who built the agent, and who has accepted none of it in writing.*

# THE EXAMINATION YOU ALREADY RAN

Five chapters in this book assigned you a piece of homework. Read together, the five assignments are not reading exercises. They are a miniature reconciliation of your own tenant, and if you ran them as you went, you have already produced the first draft of the finding an examiner would write. Collected here for the reader who wants to run them in one sitting.

One. Pull up the busiest agent in your tenant and produce the name of the human who put a signature on it before deployment. Not the builder, not the operating team, not the executive who would take the blame. (Chapter 1)

Two. Run the four interviews. Ask the builder, the business owner, the platform team, and compliance who is accountable for one deployed agent, separately, and compare the answers. (Chapter 2)

Three. Look up the oldest flow in your environment and read its created date. Then read it as a governance document. (Chapter 6)

Four. Open one agent identity in the admin center and read the sponsor field. Then ask whether the named person ever decided anything, and whether any record could show it. (Chapter 12)

Five. Find your tenant's oldest authorization and the date on its signature. Then count the changes since that date that carried no duty to reopen it. (Chapter 15)

Whatever these five produced is your organization's answer to the question on the cover, as of tonight. The forty minutes are in Chapter 20.

# SOURCES

Every factual claim in this book is sourced in the chapter where it appears, by name and date, in the sentence or beside it. That was a design decision, not a formatting one: a reader standing in front of an examiner does not have time to flip to the back. This section consolidates each chapter's sources in one place for the reader who wants to pull a primary record, verify a capability claim against the documentation page it cites, or check whether a dated claim still holds. Platform documentation entries carry the date the page was verified; the claim is warranted as of that date and no further.

Chapter 1: The Examiner Walks In. Microsoft service health advisory CW1226324 (February 3, 2026; advisory text publicly preserved via the UK NHS support portal repost and carried verbatim by The Register, February 18, 2026, "Copilot Chat bug bypasses DLP on 'Confidential' email"; also per white paper v1, Zenodo 10.5281/zenodo.20481551); FINRA, "Emerging Trend in GenAI: Observations on AI Agents" (January 2026); Moffatt v. Air Canada, 2024 BCCRT 149 (decided February 14, 2024, verified July 5, 2026); Microsoft Entra Agent ID product status (Microsoft Learn, verified July 9, 2026); Agent 365 GA May 1, 2026 (per The

Governance Gap, May 12, 2026 edition, and Learn what's-new page, verified July 9, 2026).

Chapter 2: The Accountability Assumption in Microsoft Environments. Cisco Cloud Consumption Service shadow IT measurement, Bob Dimicco, January 2013 to July 2015, and January 2016 follow-up (Cisco blogs, August 19, 2015 and January 2016, verified July 5, 2026); Mobley v. Workday, Inc., No. 3:23-cv-00770-RFL, N.D. Cal., filed February 21, 2023; agent-theory ruling July 2024; preliminary collective certification May 16, 2025; court-authorized notice February 17, 2026 to applicants 40+ since September 24, 2020; discovery status per Duane Morris class action defense blog summaries of the May 29, 2026 discovery order and June 22, 2026 motion-to-dismiss order; Entra agent identity object model; owner/sponsor distinction and sponsor definition; Copilot Studio auto-registration with creator as sponsor; sponsor lifecycle workflows and owner/sponsor/manager administrative relationships (Microsoft Learn, verified July 9, 2026).

Chapter 3: Why Microsoft Defaults Don't Answer Who Owns the Agent. Purview unified audit log capture of Copilot interactions with file references and sensitivity labels; prompt/response storage in the user mailbox with eDiscovery and legal hold; DSPM for AI transcript retrieval; Copilot Studio logging to Purview; Entra Agent ID authentication logging; Copilot Control System license-tier split (Microsoft Learn, four pages, verified August 13, 2026:
learn.microsoft.com/en-us/purview/audit-copilot,
/purview/ai-m365-copilot,
/microsoft-copilot-studio/admin-logging-copilot-studio,

/microsoft-365/copilot/copilot-control-system/security-governance). Entra agent identity object model: agent identities, blueprints, agent users. Owner/sponsor roles and sponsor accountability for purpose and lifecycle. Owner/sponsor/manager administrative relationships and sponsor lifecycle workflows (Microsoft Learn, verified July 9, 2026). Agent 365 general availability May 1, 2026 and Entra Agent ID capabilities included for agents managed by Agent 365 (Microsoft Learn what's-new, verified July 9, 2026). Agent Governance Toolkit: released April 2, 2026, MIT license, runtime policy engine intercepting agent actions, SDKs in Python, TypeScript, .NET, Rust, Go, developer-adopted per-agent (Microsoft Open Source Blog, opensource.microsoft.com/blog/2026/04/02/introducing-the-agent-governance-toolkit-open-source-runtime-security-for-ai-agents/, web-verified August 13, 2026; independent corroboration Help Net Security, April 3, 2026). Business Central Sales Order Agent acting under its own user ID with actions in history and posted documents. AI shared responsibility model (Microsoft Learn, learn.microsoft.com/en-us/azure/security/fundamentals/shared-responsibility-ai, web-verified August 13, 2026). Customer AI governance and oversight obligations including SaaS deployments (Microsoft Learn service assurance, learn.microsoft.com/en-us/compliance/assurance/assurance-artificial-intelligence, web-verified August 13, 2026).

Chapter 4: Microsoft 365 Copilot. EchoLeak / CVE-2025-32711: Aim Security (Aim Labs) discovery and disclosure, June 2025; CVSS 9.3 critical; Microsoft MSRC advisory wording "AI command injection in M365 Copilot"; server-side fix, no customer action, no known in-the-wild exploitation (SecurityWeek, June 12, 2025; The Hacker News, June 2025; MSRC advisory CVE-2025-32711; all web-verified July 10, 2026). Copilot permission enforcement, including view and extract rights on encrypted content: Microsoft Learn data protection architecture page (learn.microsoft.com/en-us/copilot/microsoft-365/microsoft-365-copilot-architecture-data-protection-auditing, verified August 13, 2026). Oversharing blueprint (pilot/deploy/operate), DSPM for AI risk assessments, SharePoint Advanced Management included with the Copilot license, Content Management Assessment, site access reviews, Restricted Access Control, Restricted Content Discovery as temporary site-level control, DLP exclusion from Copilot grounding: Microsoft Learn (learn.microsoft.com/en-us/copilot/microsoft-365/microsoft-365-copilot-blueprint-oversharing; /en-us/sharepoint/restricted-content-discovery; /en-us/microsoft-365/copilot/configure-secure-governed-data-foundation-microsoft-365-copilot; /en-us/sharepoint/get-ready-copilot-sharepoint-advanced-management; all verified July 10, 2026; blueprint controls re-verified August 13, 2026). Restricted SharePoint Search retirement, new enablement blocked July 31, 2026, removed from print accordingly (learn.microsoft.com/sharepoint/restricted-sharepoint-search, verified August 13, 2026).

Chapter 5: Copilot Studio Agents. Zenity/Bargury Black Hat USA 2024: "15 Ways to Break Your Copilot," Michael Bargury, CTO, Zenity; internet scan finding tens of thousands of Copilot

Studio agents publicly reachable without authentication due to then-default publish settings; Microsoft default change applying to new deployments only; CopilotHunter release; Bargury crediting Microsoft's responsiveness (The Register, August 8, 2024). More than 1,000 exposed agents attributed to Fortune 500 companies with sensitive data extraction demonstrated, including legal documents (Zenity Labs research summary of Black Hat USA 2024 publications, labs.zenity.io). Near-3,000 agents per average large enterprise and majority-discoverable figures attributed in print as vendor figures via The Register (August 8, 2024). Automatic agent identity creation with creator recorded as sponsor: Microsoft Learn, learn.microsoft.com/en-us/entra/agent-id/what-are-agent-identities (verified August 13, 2026). March 18, 2026 start of automatic identity creation for new agents in enabled environments; environment-level opt-out since closed, agent identities mandatory for all new agents from July 2026; legacy agents on platform-managed service principals treated as standard applications; recreate-and-decommission as the only migration path: Microsoft Learn, learn.microsoft.com/en-us/entra/agent-id/migrate-copilot-studio-agents-to-agent-id and learn.microsoft.com/en-us/microsoft-copilot-studio/admin-use-entra-agent-identities (verified August 13, 2026). Entra ID Governance machinery for agent identities (deliberate sponsor assignment, access packages, expiry-driven sponsor extension or lapse decisions): learn.microsoft.com/en-us/entra/id-governance/agent-id-governance-overview (verified August 13, 2026). "Some preexisting agents might not have sponsors yet" and sponsor-with-limited-permissions detail:

learn.microsoft.com/en-us/microsoft-copilot-studio/requirements-certificates-configuration-values (verified August 13, 2026). Event triggers, maker-credential authentication for autonomous operation in default configurations, pre-publish warning, admin ability to block triggers: learn.microsoft.com/en-us/microsoft-copilot-studio/authoring-triggers-about (verified August 13, 2026). Control maker credential options (per environment or environment group, not enabled by default; blocking maker credentials requires a live user sign-in per tool call and "all agent triggers must involve an active user"): learn.microsoft.com/en-us/microsoft-copilot-studio/configure-no-maker-authentication (verified August 13, 2026). Sharing controls via Managed Environments and environment groups: learn.microsoft.com/en-us/microsoft-copilot-studio/admin-sharing-controls-limits (verified August 13, 2026). Tenant-wide disable of generative AI agent publishing: learn.microsoft.com/en-us/microsoft-copilot-studio/security-and-governance (verified August 13, 2026). Connector API permissions attached to the agent identity at publish: learn.microsoft.com/en-us/microsoft-copilot-studio/admin-use-entra-agent-identities (verified August 13, 2026). Agent Registry in the Microsoft 365 admin center listing name, creator, creation date, host products, availability: learn.microsoft.com/en-us/microsoft-365/admin/manage/manage-copilot-agents-integrated-apps (verified August 13, 2026).

Chapter 6: Power Platform Automation. UpGuard Research disclosure "By Design: How Default Permissions on Microsoft Power Apps Exposed Millions," published August 23, 2021 (upguard.com/breaches/power-apps); The Register, August 23,

2021 (affected-entity list, no-public-misuse statement, Microsoft payroll portal figures); TechRepublic, August 23-25, 2021 ("considered to be by design" wording, June 24 MSRC report date, June 29 case closure, Microsoft spokesperson response, default change and diagnostic tool). Microsoft Learn: manage orphaned flows (learn.microsoft.com/en-us/troubleshoot/power-platform/power-automate/flow-management/manage-orphan-flow-when-owner-leaves-org); flow ownership models including service principal recommendation and "continue to run smoothly even if employees leave the company" (learn.microsoft.com/en-us/power-automate/guidance/coding-guidelines/understand-access-to-flows); cloud flow sharing, co-owner powers, shared-connection scope (learn.microsoft.com/en-us/power-automate/create-team-flows); CoE Starter Kit orphaned-objects governance process, manager-routing and disposition menu (learn.microsoft.com/en-us/power-platform/guidance/coe/governance-components). All Learn pages verified August 13, 2026. The CoE orphaned-objects manager menu (take ownership / reassign / delete / list) corroborated against Microsoft Learn use-governance-components and setup-orphan-components pages; the CoE Starter Kit's 2026 move off active maintenance, with capabilities folding into the Power Platform admin center, is covered in the companion annex.

Chapter 7: Azure AI and Microsoft Foundry Custom Agents. NYC Mayor's Office, press release No. 777-23, "Mayor Adams Releases First-of-Its-Kind Plan for Responsible Artificial Intelligence Use in New York City Government," October 16, 2023 (nyc.gov); The Markup, "NYC's AI Chatbot Tells Businesses to

Break the Law," Colin Lecher, March 29, 2024, co-published with THE CITY and Documented (themarkup.org/artificial-intelligence/2024/03/29/nycs-ai-chatbot-tells-businesses-to-break-the-law); THE CITY co-publication of the same investigation (Microsoft declined comment; thirty-day data deletion); THE CITY and The Markup, April 2, 2024 (bot stays up; disclaimer wording); The Markup and THE CITY, "Mamdani to kill the NYC AI chatbot," Colin Lecher and Katie Honan, January 30, 2026, with February 4, 2026 update (termination, "functionally unusable," reported ~$600,000 build cost, "beta test has ended"). Microsoft Learn pages as listed in the accuracy section, verified August 13, 2026. SR 26-2, Board of Governors of the Federal Reserve System, OCC, FDIC, April 17, 2026 (federalreserve.gov/supervisionreg/srletters/SR2602.htm and SR2602.pdf; OCC Bulletin 2026-13). SHRM, "NYC AI Chatbot Gives Faulty Legal Advice, Prompting Review," April 5, 2024 (Microsoft, "which runs the chatbot with Azure AI, said it is working with city officials to improve its accuracy and alignment with official paperwork").

Chapter 8: Agent 365 and the Orchestration Layer. Microsoft 365 Blog, "Microsoft Agent 365: The control plane for AI agents," November 18, 2025 (microsoft.com/en-us/microsoft-365/blog/2025/11/18/microsoft-agent-365-the-control-plane-for-ai-agents/). Microsoft Learn, all verified July 10, 2026: Agent 365 overview (GA May 1, 2026); agent registry admin page (tiles, risk taxonomy, filters, Graph API preview, Excel export); agent registry convergence; agent actions (assign new owner, block, delete); agent map; agent details

(Connected Agents tab); connect existing agents (registry sync preview); why an enterprise needs Agent 365 (agent sprawl usage); Microsoft 365 Admin agent; FastTrack for Microsoft Agent 365; Agent 365 integration with Foundry (five pillars, access control); Office 365 service descriptions for Microsoft Agent 365 (licensing and feature tiers). Copilot Studio and Foundry identity facts by pointer to the Ch 5 and Ch 7 verified records.

Chapter 9: Multi-Agent Scenarios and Chain Authorization. FINRA, "Emerging Trend in GenAI: Observations on AI Agents," Greg Ruppert, January 27, 2026 (finra.org/media-center/blog/observations-on-ai-agents, verified July 10, 2026). NIST, "Announcing the AI Agent Standards Initiative for Interoperable and Secure Innovation," February 17, 2026 (nist.gov, verified July 10, 2026). ASD's ACSC, CISA, NSA, and Five Eyes partner agencies, "Careful Adoption of Agentic AI Services," May 1, 2026 (cisa.gov resource page, verified July 10, 2026). SR 26-2, Board of Governors of the Federal Reserve System, OCC, FDIC, April 17, 2026. Microsoft Learn, verified July 10, 2026: connect an agent over the Agent2Agent (A2A) protocol (add-agent-agent-to-agent); agent identities in Microsoft Entra Agent ID (agent-identities); Copilot Studio blog, multi-agent capabilities to general availability (spring 2026). By pointer to prior verified records: Purview audit surfaces (Ch 3), maker-credential triggers, flow connections, Agent Map and Connected Agents tab (Ch 8).

Chapter 10: The Authorization Layer. Royal Commission into the Robodebt Scheme, final report and media release, July 7, 2023 (robodebt.royalcommission.gov.au/publications/report, verified

July 5, 2026). Australian Public Service Commission, Robodebt Centralised Code of Conduct Inquiry, Commissioner's statement and Taskforce final report, September 13, 2024 (apsc.gov.au; carries the sixteen-referrals count and its current-and-former composition verbatim). Regulation (EU) 2024/1689 as amended by the Digital Omnibus (Council final approval June 29, 2026; verified July 11, 2026 against contemporaneous legal analyses including Gibson Dunn, White & Case, and DLA Piper client alerts). SR 26-2, Federal Reserve, OCC, FDIC, April 17, 2026. Microsoft Foundry Blog, June 2, 2026 (devblogs.microsoft.com/foundry/build-2026-open-trust-stack-ai-agents/, verified August 13, 2026).

Chapter 11: Intent Architecture for Microsoft Deployments. Zillow Group Q3 2021 shareholder letter, 8-K exhibit, November 2, 2021 (sec.gov primary record, re-fetched July 11, 2026). NIST NCCoE draft concept paper, "Accelerating the Adoption of Software and AI Agent Identity and Authorization," February 5, 2026, public comment through April 2, 2026 (primary PDF fetched July 11, 2026). Microsoft Learn sponsor schema and administrative-relationship pages (verified July 4 and July 9, 2026).

Chapter 12: Microsoft Entra Agent ID and What Identity Doesn't Solve. Platform citations print inline in this chapter, each Microsoft Learn page named with its verification date at the sentence carrying the claim.

Chapter 13: Microsoft Purview as Governance Backbone (and Its Limits). Platform citations print inline in this chapter, each Microsoft Learn page named with its verification date at the sentence carrying the claim; incident material rides the verified records of the chapters that established it.

Chapter 14: Tenant Agent Reconciliation in Microsoft Environments. Cyber Safety Review Board, Review of the December 2021 Log4j Event, published July 11, 2022 (cisa.gov primary PDF, verified July 5, 2026): the no-comprehensive-list finding and quoted sub-system clause, the 33,000-hour figure, the endemic-vulnerability conclusion, the inventory-and-SBOM recommendations. Microsoft Learn agent registry documentation by pointer to Ch 8's verified record (July 10, 2026). Chapter 5's cutover record and Chapter 6's flow-fleet record by pointer. The framework library's rogue-employees observation, attributed in print. Microsoft Entra Tenant Governance general availability: Microsoft Entra blog, techcommunity.microsoft.com, August 10, 2026; capability detail per the Tenant Governance overview, learn.microsoft.com/entra/id-governance/tenant-governance/overview, verified August 13, 2026.

Chapter 15: Authorization Coverage Lifecycle Across Microsoft Tools. EEOC v. iTutorGroup, Inc., No. 1:22-cv-2565 (E.D.N.Y.), primary record (eeoc.gov, verified July 5, 2026): the rejection rules, the 200-plus figure, the resubmission detection, the August 9, 2023 filing and September 8, 2023 consent decree approval, the 365,000 dollars and five years of monitoring; the chair's position paraphrased without quotation marks. Upstart Holdings Model 22: launch May 2025, Q3 2025 conversion decline 23.9 to 20.6 percent, November 4, 2025 earnings-call characterizations (overly responsive; calibrated more conservatively), twenty-million-dollar guidance cut, 9.71 percent share decline November 5, 2025, corroborated against contemporaneous reporting (Banking Dive, April 10, 2026; Pomerantz LLP announcement; Levi & Korsinsky notices) and consistent with the author's white paper record; Dunn v. Upstart Holdings, Inc., No. 3:26-cv-02974 (N.D. Cal., filed April 7, 2026) cited per the white paper's PACER-verified record with the no-merits-ruling caution printed. SR 26-2 (April 17, 2026). All Microsoft facts by pointer to prior chapters' verified records; no new Learn citations required or made.

Chapter 16: The Disposition Protocol and Microsoft Signal Sources. SEC order In the Matter of Knight Capital Americas LLC, Exchange Act Release No. 70694 (October 16, 2013) and SEC press release 2013-222, primary records verified (sec.gov). Massachusetts Attorney General press release (July 10, 2025) and the Earnest assurance of discontinuance (Suffolk County Superior Court), both primary records read in full (verified July 2026). Agent Governance Toolkit release facts (Microsoft Open Source Blog, April 2, 2026, verified July 2026). All other Microsoft facts by pointer to prior chapters' verified records.

Chapter 17: The Agent Governance Toolkit and What It Cannot Prove. Agent Governance Toolkit open-source release, April 2, 2026, MIT license (Microsoft Open Source Blog, per Chapter 3's record). Microsoft Tech Community posts on the toolkit: architecture deep dive, April 10, 2026; shift-left governance, May 1, 2026; "After the Agent Acts: Proving What Happened and Who Authorized It," May 14, 2026 (techcommunity.microsoft.com, all verified August 13, 2026, including the require_approval parameters against the deep dive's own code sample and the eleven-word accountability-gap quotation against the May 14 post). The toolkit's own OWASP Agentic Security Initiative coverage mapping, seven full, three partial, zero gaps (microsoft.github.io/agent-governance-toolkit/compliance/owasp-agentic-top10-architecture/, verified August 13, 2026).

Chapter 18: Agent Authorization Document for Microsoft Deployments. Moffatt v. Air Canada, 2024 BCCRT 149, by pointer to Chapter 1's record; SR 26-2, April 17, 2026, by pointer to Chapter 7's record; Microsoft Learn facts by pointer to Chapters 5 and 12 (verified July 10 and 11, 2026). No new citations introduced.

Chapter 19: The Examiner Returns. This chapter introduces no new citations; every claim rides a prior chapter's sourced record, and the seven questions print verbatim from Chapter 1.

Chapter 20: Forty Minutes That Prevent Four Months. This chapter introduces no new citations, no capability claims, and no statistics; both duration figures are labeled estimates in the prose itself.

# ACKNOWLEDGMENTS

This book began as a newsletter question that would not stay answered. The readers of The Governance Gap asked the versions of it that made the frameworks sharper, and several of them will recognize their objections in these chapters, upgraded into arguments.

To Nabanita, who made room in a shared life for a book that kept expanding to fill it, and to Sayan, the thanks that a page can carry and the debt that it cannot.

The errors that survived all of this verification are the author's, and the corrections page for them is the companion annex.

---

# ABOUT THE AUTHOR

Sougata Roy writes about enterprise AI governance from the perspective of the person who has to sign for it. He has spent thirteen years on federal engagements at United States agencies including the Securities and Exchange Commission, the Commodity Futures Trading Commission, and the National Institutes of Health, environments where the question of who authorized a system is not rhetorical and the answer is expected in writing.

He is the author of The Governance Gap, a weekly newsletter on AI accountability in Microsoft enterprise environments, where much of this book's vocabulary was worked out in public. His prior publications include the white paper Who Owns the Agent? (May 2026) and The Authorization Layer, a library of fifteen governance frameworks (July 2026), both openly deposited and both extended by this book.

He can be found at sougataroy.com, where the frameworks in these pages live in their maintained form.

# THE COMPANION ANNEX

The fast-moving half of this book lives online, exactly as the note at the front promised. The companion annex maintains, against current Microsoft documentation: console procedures and admin center paths, license tier names and plan boundaries, preview statuses, the capability details the chapters deliberately kept out of print, and corrections to this edition.

The annex is at sougataroy.com/who-owns-the-agent-annex.

The blank Agent Authorization Record in Appendix A is there too, in a form you can complete. The date on which you first open it is worth noticing. Most organizations discover the form takes less time to complete than the meeting about who should complete it took to schedule.

www.ingramcontent.com/pod-product-compliance
Lightning Source LLC
LaVergne TN
LVHW100725061126
851857LV00011B/403
* 9 7 9 8 9 9 7 1 9 8 3 0 5 *